Balboa Press books may be ordered through booksellers or by contacting:

Balboa Press
A Division of Hay House
1663 Liberty Drive
Bloomington, IN 47403
www.balboapress.com
1-(877) 407-4847

Because of the dynamic nature of the Internet, any web addresses or links contained in this book may have changed since publication and may no longer be valid. The views expressed in this work are solely those of the author and do not necessarily reflect the views of the publisher, and the publisher hereby disclaims any responsibility for them.

ISBN: 978-1-4525-4517-2 (sc)
ISBN: 978-1-4525-4519-6 (hc)
ISBN: 978-1-4525-4518-9 (e)
Library of Congress Control Number: 2012900143

The author of this book does not dispense medical advice or prescribe the use of any technique as a form of treatment for physical, emotional, or medical problems without the advice of a physician, either directly or indirectly. The intent of the author is only to offer information of a general nature to help you in your quest for emotional and spiritual well-being. In the event you use any of the information in this book for yourself, which is your constitutional right, the author and the publisher assume no responsibility for your actions.

Any people depicted in stock imagery provided by Thinkstock are models, and such images are being used for illustrative purposes only.
Certain stock imagery © Thinkstock.

Printed in the United States of America

Balboa Press rev. date: 3/05/2012

FINDING THE LIGHT

How to achieve inner peace
by forgiving past and present life traumas

Liz Vincent

BALBOA.
PRESS
A DIVISION OF HAY HOUSE

This book is dedicated to:

My father Cliff Vincent, my cousin Warwick
Pugh, my friend Wally Widdicombe and to Bella
my dog, all of whom I loved very much

Acknowledgements

I would also like to say thank you for all the love and support I have received from the following people whilst writing this book:

To my mother for always being there and for helping me to make this possible. My great friend Cari Edwards and my lovely neighbour Philip de Bary for tirelessly helping me with corrections, improvements and the synopsis. Victor Richard Stockinger who helped me to get started in Harley Street. To my friends Nick Edwards, Gillian Widdicombe, Anita Lohne, Matthew Clark, David Rosenthal, Sally Dutton, Chris M Smith, Tim Ross, Susan Pugh, Tracey Smythe, Fiona Brake, Claire Allen (now Phillips), Alixa McIntosh, Carol Screen, Samantha Nutbeen and Dee Rendall for all helping me in different ways. My aunt Peggy Pugh for completely trusting in me and my work, and Sergio Scifoni for being there encouraging me every time I have an emotional wobble.

For all the computer help given to me by Julian and Lawrence Widdicombe and also my brother Richard Vincent. I would also like to say a very special thank you to Julian Widdicombe for creating my fantastic website. To Ben, Kay and James Vincent for always being supportive. I would also like to say a huge thank you to my friends in America – Judy Pastore, Amy Venezian and Monica Bautista, plus a special thank you to Rita Mae Brown for writing the foreword.

Liz Vincent

Contents

Foreword

Past lives? Isn't this one bad enough?

When Judy Pastore, former producer of *The Roseanne Show*, an American TV show, suggested I met Liz Vincent, I demurred. Not that I wasn't willing to meet an English lady, for I adore the English and have always been well treated when in our mother country, but regression, hypnosis? However, Judy, apart from being beautiful, is also persuasive. I relented.

Just to be sure, I brought along two friends: one a former army major and emergency room doctor and another, a Smith College graduate with her PhD working as a botanist; two scientists who would provide ballast just in case I lurched too far to port and, since I'm a writer, could be accused of too much imagination. What I really am is a farmer born and bred but I can hardly make a penny at it. That's a long story and I fear it's the same in many countries now. But still, past life regression?

Meeting Liz, all three of us felt warmth, good humour and strength of character. She didn't look like a wing nut. She didn't act like a lunatic. Nor did she appear in star spangled robes with a tall cap like the magician in *Fantasia*.

What the hell? Give it a shot.

The army major went first, which an army major should do in most circumstances. When I returned to Judy's cottage in central

Virginia, which we call the Yellow Teacup, to collect her, I noticed she was unusually quiet. The next shift walked upstairs with Liz and I took my friend, who had flown in from Nevada, home. Physicians may be chatty although I haven't found too many to be so, but when you combine an MD with army leadership, best to keep a tight lip.

I asked, "How did it go?" and a torrent followed, tears, laughter and insight. I could find no signs of alcohol and while it was early in the day that doesn't necessarily stop some folks. No, stone cold sober, clear headed and my major just went on and on. The result was a peace, an understanding, a release of useless emotions.

The same thing happened when I returned to pick up the scientist who has spent her entire life being logical, using the scientific method, defending her results. Her world is particularly closed to forms of experience or knowledge which cannot be weighted, measured, proved. Shaken, in tears and sometimes sobbing, the experience challenged her basis for apprehending reality. Yes, she saw old friends, deceased family in different forms in different times, but the real jolt was the vivid demonstration that we live in a culture that denies so much. We blow it off as touchy feely, crackpot and we aren't far off from gutting the arts either, since how can one prove a symphony and why bother to write one anyway? What do the arts have to do with the bottom line?

To some extent, this, too, was my feeling except that I love the arts. Seeing the response of two dear friends, I wondered what I would encounter. Once upstairs, Liz made one comfortable and spoke a bit. She asks you to put yourself in a hall. She may ask other people to put themselves in other places. One gets to open doors in the hall. What a time I had throwing open doors. I expected nothing but there I was somewhere else, experiencing, in my case, far too much war but being oddly exhilarated. Nor was I afraid of my deaths which I was asked to recount. At no time was I led, was anything suggested to me. This stuff just poured out of me. Exciting as it is, it's also exhausting and Liz had a keen sense of when to bring one back to the present. However, I didn't want to come back because, in my last recollection, I was a large hound dog, a foxhound, and I loved my kennelmates, loved my huntsman, loved the huntsman's little daughter, and loved, loved, loved the chase. My nose filled with such scents, I could run so fast and with the horses. My purpose was clear and I loved a rousing good life. Liz had a bit of work to bring me back and I was, at first, bitterly disappointed. I didn't want to be human, a point my enemies will be sure to seize upon.

I have never been so happy as during that recollection. I asked Liz if other people have animal lives. She said a few, not too many.

From the time I was tiny I got along with animals but most especially foxhounds since my grandfather and great uncle had packs of them. People often comment on my relationship with my hounds and I reply I don't know what I know, we just click. Perhaps now I know.

But what Liz has taught me and countless others is to suspend judgement, listen to your heart and realise the light is within. That light is within you, cats, dogs, horses, and hounds – all living creatures I believe. We share this earth together and if we can't cooperate (I don't wish to be a lion's lunch) at least give every creature his due.

May this book give you insight, lead you towards what your tasks are, what burdens you need to put down, but most of all may you recognise and honour your own light.

Always and Ever

Rita Mae Brown, MFH, Ph.D.

Preface: Looking for the Light

As I walked into my new treatment room at number One Harley Street London my first thought was: "Oh my gosh, I've done it. I've finally arrived".

My journey to get me to the most prestigious medical street in England and possibly in the world started in a rather odd and humble way.

I am not a doctor, nor have I ever been trained in other forms of conventional medicine. I am an experienced hypnotherapist who specialises, with the use of many different techniques I have learnt along the way, in past life regression and deep emotional healing.

So, what am I doing in Harley Street? I am here because many people are now exploring new, different and exciting methods of healing. Doctors, paramedics and nurses are dedicated people doing a fantastic job of saving lives every day of the week. Unfortunately the system often breaks down because many medical practitioners look at medicine only in the conventional western way. They give medication to solve immediate problems but rarely examine the root cause of why the patient contracted the illness in the first place. The body is treated as a separate entity from the mind and the reasons why the patient contracts the illness in the first place are largely ignored. This is not a criticism of doctors – it is just the way the system works. They just do not have the time to listen to their patients' emotional problems, which could help to prevent illness developing.

The patient is always taught that it is the doctor who is healing them. This is not quite true. They are actually allowing themselves to heal as a result of the belief they have in the doctor and the belief they have in the medicine prescribed.

Hypnotherapy is a means of allowing clients to connect to their own subconscious minds. Therefore it is a method that allows everyone to understand what is held deeply within them. Used correctly it is also a way for us to release all of the negative emotions we hold in our mind, body and soul.

Ever since I was a child I have been intuitive, with a powerful imagination. My dreams were vivid and I often saw what I believed to be angels. For many years whilst living in Italy I had been devouring all the books I could find on the spirit world and on past life regression. It was really important to me to find out how people such as Brian Weiss, Sylvia Browne, Dolores Cannon and Hans Tendam worked. They were all getting amazing results with both physical and psychological problems using past life regression. The spark was ignited in me and the more I read on the subject the more I knew that this was what I really wanted to do.

In order to become a past life regression therapist I needed to train as a hypnotherapist. Very few people were teaching past life regression at the time because very few hypnotherapists were using it. There also seemed to be a general fear around the subject. Most schools of hypnotherapy did not consider past life regression work to be part of the curriculum. Therefore it was very important for me to find someone to teach me who was not only a hypnotherapist, but a past life regression therapist. Luckily I found Ursula Markham, who was one of the very few practising past life therapists at that time. She had also written a book on the subject. Ursula was about to retire but I was lucky enough to be trained by her before she handed her school over to someone else.

Early on in my career I was also extremely fortunate to attend a seminar given by Ormond McGill. He was 92 when I met him and was known as the Dean of American Hypnosis. That man could just look at you and you would go into trance. He was amazing and, at my request, he demonstrated past life regression. It was the most fascinating thing I have ever seen. The very British lady he chose to work with instantly became a 19th-century Frenchwoman, accent and all. I was mesmerised and realised that I had finally found my true calling.

He ran the seminar with Tom Silver, who is another great American hypnotherapist. Tom uses fast techniques to get people into instant hypnosis and he often hypnotises whole groups at a time. This was also invaluable to me as at the time I was only aware of English methods, which are much slower and more time consuming.

Over the next few years I trained in Hypnotherapy, Past Life Regression, CBT, NLP, EFT, EmoTrance, Tachyon Healing, EMDR, Reiki, Seichem Healing, Spirit Release Therapy and Theta Healing. I also went to college and trained to become a teacher. More recently I have studied Matrix Energetics and Hawaiian Hooponopono. Life has truly become a journey of discovery.

In order to understand things on a deeper level I also felt that it was necessary to develop my psychic abilities. For many years, whenever I was in England I had visited the spiritualist church and sat in mediumship circles. One of my reasons for leaving Italy was to understand more about this side of myself, which at that time I felt unable to do without the support of more like-minded people. Now I no longer attend the spiritualist church because I feel that my studies have taken me far away from any conventional church beliefs. However, I shall always be grateful for everything I learnt there as it really pushed my psychic abilities forward, together with a two-year clairvoyant course at Hartcliffe College in Bristol.

Once my hypnotherapy qualifications were in place, I started to build up my practice. I realise now, thankfully, that I never actually had any self doubt. I was confident in what I was doing and absolutely determined to be the best in my field. Many people have since told me that it took years for them to build up a practice and, indeed, some never really do manage to work full time with their chosen occupation. I qualified, got myself up on the web and started seeing clients.

For the first few months I continued to work in sales for three days a week so that I could guarantee an income. I saw clients in Bristol on the other days. Luckily, after three months, I was able to give up the sales job and work just as a full-time therapist.

My goal was always to be in London, Harley Street. Then after a while through a friend of a friend, another hypnotherapist invited me to use his Harley Street room for one day a week. It was a start!

Gradually the practice began to build and when the man whose office I was using decided to move back to Scotland he gave me first refusal on the space. So, within a year I had my own Harley Street practice. I invited a good friend to join me and now we share the room. I still work between London and Bristol and he also has a second practice so it works out well for both of us.

Chapter 1:   Past Life Work

Past life work is not really about seeing lives and then travelling to old cemeteries to find your gravestone or even about proving you have lived before. It is about releasing and letting go of old negative patterns and emotions.

The more I worked with conventional past life therapy the more I realised how much more there was to it, and how many different techniques could be added to enable the client to get so much more from the experience.

Harmful emotions

We hold so much anger and resentment within our bodies and souls. When we feel angry at someone, we are really only angry at ourselves. That person is just mirroring something deeply negative within us in order for us to resolve it. Once this emotion is understood it can be released so that we are liberated. When we work to clear our deeply rooted anger we are set free to create much happier and more positive lives for ourselves.

We constantly blame other people for situations that we ourselves create. Therefore it is really important for us to realise how this affects us. We need to know how to resolve and release these negative harmful emotions.

Understanding this has led to the development of my own way of working, which incorporates spirit release, releasing old oaths and vows, tie cutting, forgiveness and soul retrieval all in a single session.

Physical illnesses are usually caused by anger, resentment, guilt, fear and shock. All of these emotions affect our immune system and our natural ability to fight disease. If you break down the word into its true meaning it becomes clear that dis-ease is when our body is not at ease with itself in some way.

Our job as individuals or souls is to let go of all the old hurts and resentments that we so desperately hold on to. We are all guilty of holding on to a great deal of rubbish. I had to go through what is sometimes termed "the dark night of the soul" to emerge as a much stronger and more balanced person. There is still work to do because this is a never ending process, but I know that I am now almost where I want to be. I am a much stronger human being since clearing out so many of my negative beliefs and emotions.

Every time we come into this world we decide what it is we need to experience in order for our souls to grow. We choose our parents, we choose our relations and we choose our lovers. All because, on a deeper level, we know that these are the people best suited to help us mirror all of the stuff that we are harbouring deep within our subconscious minds – those negative emotions that we need to recognise and clear out of our psyche. Therefore, when we know and understand this, we also begin to grasp the fact that the buck stops with us.

We meet people lifetime after lifetime because we keep on repeating the same errors until we finally recognise what is going on. Then when we get the message we forgive, let go and move on.

When I visit past lives, or parallel lives as they are sometimes called, with my clients we often find that they have oaths and vows tying them etherically together with one or many people. These can be vows of love but more often they are vows of hatred and vengeance.

How often have you met someone you were instantly attracted to or who you immediately disliked? When this happens you can bet your life that there is some unfinished business between you both.

When I was on an advanced EFT course some years ago I remember feeling an instant dislike for an Irish nurse who was sitting a few feet away from me. I had never spoken to this woman but something about her made me feel very uncomfortable. Luckily for me she was much more evolved than I was at the time and, during the break, she came up to me and said that we had some unfinished business to sort out.

I was quite taken aback and rather ashamed by this because I knew she could feel my irrational dislike of her. I agreed to work with her and as I did so I immediately saw myself working as a doctor during the Crimean war. My psychic training has left me with the ability to instantly tune into my past lives when I need to, so this was one case in point. The picture I saw was of me as a man quite short and balding, who was over worked, stressed and forced to do many amputations. Due to limited sanitation and the amount of gangrene and infections on the wards at that time, life was very hard for all of us. She was my head nurse and very bossy. We did not like one another at all probably due to overwork, the stench and death all around us. As she started to tune in and to remember we hugged, started laughing and completely forgave ourselves and one another for all the animosity between us. I spent the rest of the course thinking what a nice woman she was. Oh, the power of forgiveness!

Forgiveness

This to me was absolute living proof of how important forgiveness is. It allows us to be free from our past so we can move forward. Perhaps this is quite an odd example, but I have found myself in other similar situations and if I ask to be shown what the feelings

3

are about, I can always release whatever it is and let it go. Once we can let go of any animosity towards other individuals our lives will very quickly change for the better.

When I work with my clients doing past life regressions I always help them to clear up any forgiveness. This allows unfinished business to be sorted out and is especially important if the person has been wounded, hurt or killed by someone in a previous life. It is interesting to note that if you ask the client to forgive the perpetrator in that past life, they frequently say that they will never forgive them. However, if the client is told to lift their awareness and to travel into the spirit world after that lifetime, they are more able to forgive.

Very often we leave behind in our past lives soul fragments, those broken off parts of us which are so angry they are still hanging around; they continue to influence our behaviour in a negative way today. When this is the case it is important that the soul fragment is moved into the light where it can be healed. Then all the oaths and vows we have made can be cleared so that absolute forgiveness can take place.

Sometimes these fragments need to stay in the spirit world and sometimes they need to come back. The client will always know what is best for them. I believe that when the client feels the need for the fragment to come back it is because that piece can help them to understand, or remember, important lessons or give them some form of strength. When they feel that it needs to stay in the spirit world it is of no use to the client at this time.

Forgiveness is always a three-way process. We need to forgive in every way the person who we believe has hurt us; we need to ask them to forgive us for all the negative energy we have been sending out towards them. Then we need to completely forgive ourselves for what has happened to us. In cases where the client finds it difficult to forgive someone, I get them to forgive themselves first. Once this has been achieved, the client finds it much easier to forgive the person who has hurt them. They will usually say something like: "Oh well, I might as well forgive them, mightn't I?", when a few minutes before they would have been adamant that they would never, ever, forgive the person for what they had done.

Taking responsibility

Of course people are not always prepared to work on themselves. It is so much easier to blame outside situations and other people for everything bad that happens to us. Nevertheless we will continue to be unhappy and get sick until we are prepared to take total responsibility for our own lives.

Sometimes I may see clients who, on filling out my client form, tell me that they have been to so many doctors and healers but no-one can cure them. This immediately tells me that they are not prepared to look inside themselves for a cure to their problems. Every therapist knows the type of person who really just wants to prove to themselves that every treatment they try will fail. There is usually some advantage to them holding on to whatever the malady is. It may prevent them from going to work or from taking personal responsibility in some way.

I am now inclined to be very up front and ask this type of client if they are really ready to begin taking personal responsibility for everything that has happened to them, and if they are truly ready to help me to help them improve their life. This may seem rather like shock treatment but I am no longer prepared to waste both the client's and my time with someone who is not wholly committed to helping themselves get well. It is all too easy to say: "None of this is my fault. It is all my mother's, father's, brother's, lover's fault for everything that has happened to me."

Chapter 2:   Working with Abuse

Abuse is probably the hardest thing to move on from. There are thousands and thousands of people in our society who have been on tranquilisers for long periods of time as a result of not facing and dealing with abuse issues.

It is always very difficult to forgive because anyone who suffers abuse, no matter how young they are, always believes it is their fault. It could be argued that in some way they have attracted that situation into their lives in order to work through it and forgive. But when you have seen some of the horrendous abuse cases I have worked with, even though it may be logical, it is very difficult to take on board. Abuse starts somewhere and of course from society's point of view some sort of responsibility needs to be taken by the people who cause this deep, psychologically damaging, pain.

In all of the abuse cases I have worked with, however, the abused person has been abused in one or more past lives. The person who is responsible for this is often the same person who has abused them in this lifetime.

People who have been abused find themselves stuck, very angry and unable to move on. If they are able to forgive their abuser their lives often improve quickly. Of course this is a very difficult thing to ask them to do, especially if the abuser is a family member.

I remember an interesting case of a lady who came to see me because she was very angry over the abuse she had suffered at the hands of her father. Oddly enough she was one of five sisters but the father only abused her.

We went back to a lifetime when she was the daughter of a wealthy family. She was very young, probably pretty and came from what at the time was considered an upper class privileged family. In that lifetime the man she now knows as her father was the family gardener. She didn't like the gardener because she always felt he was staring at her. Then one day, when he knew that her parents were away, he laid in wait for her and brutally raped her. When her parents returned she was too ashamed to tell them what had happened to her. She spent the rest of that lifetime hating that man and afraid of other men because of what they might do to her. She never married and lived a very lonely existence after her parents died.

Spirit agreements

What is interesting about this case is that, when I took her into the spirit world to see what she had agreed to do in this present lifetime, she told me that she and the gardener had made an agreement in this lifetime that he would be her father. She had accepted this because he wanted to make amends for how he had treated her in the past. Unfortunately this was not the way it worked out and whatever it was in her that he found irresistible in that lifetime, he still felt the same way in this. He had not been able to keep his hands off her even when she was his own daughter. It did, however, explain why she was the only child he abused.

Trying to forgive him was very difficult for her because she felt that he had not only ruined her life once before, but he had done the same again in this lifetime. There was probably much more to this actual story because we have all had thousands of past or parallel lifetimes. However, the important thing was that she achieved enough understanding of the situation to finally forgive him, since she realised that the pattern would keep repeating itself until she completely let it go.

Levels of forgiveness

It is important to forgive people on at least four levels. These are on a past life level, on a genetic level, on a physical level and on a soul level. It is also important to forgive in every dimension: thus everything gets cleared out and released once and for all.

Abuse often happens to a child in this lifetime when they were the abuser's wife in a previous life. The abuser seems to lose all rationality and will often give the excuse that they don't know why they did it, but they just couldn't help themselves. This of course does not make the abuse any less heinous, but it does sometimes help the abused person to understand the crime in a different way. It can lead to forgiveness and letting go, which enables the abused person to feel free possibly for the first time in their life.

Abuse doesn't always happen to women. Men are often abused too. One of the most horrendous cases was a man whose mother had abused him when he was a baby. She did this with the help of different men whom she brought to her bed whilst working as a prostitute. It was an obscene and shocking case, one of the most difficult I have worked on. For him to forgive her was far from easy but he did it. He is now helping his mother to turn her life around – a fantastic achievement on his part. He has moved from a deep anger towards her to unconditional love.

To help him to release this we looked at every scene until we understood what was going on with his mother at the time. She had no self worth and was a drug addict. She also had no idea how to look after a young, very vulnerable baby. She felt dirty and disgusted with herself, so did things to reinforce all these negative feelings she had inside. Once he began to understand how she felt, his sense of compassion for her grew and he was also able to begin his own healing. He was still very angry for a very long time, but the more he forgave her, the better he began to feel. Also the more he forgave himself for it having happened, the better he felt.

I have worked with clients who have been in counselling for 20 years because of abuse and after just one or two sessions clearing all of this stuff out, they are finally ready to get on with their lives.

Most of us have done some pretty terrible things in many of our lifetimes. It is about recognising and taking personal responsibility for what we have done and then forgiving ourselves for doing it. It is also about forgiving all the people in our lives who help us to learn our most difficult lessons.

Soul groups

I believe we are all part of different soul groups. We meet these same souls time and time again and it is often members of our group who help us to learn our most difficult lessons. If you had to go through a very difficult experience who would you want to go through it with – someone you trusted completely, or someone you didn't know? Well, it is the same with our life experiences. Often our most difficult lessons are taught to us by the souls we are closest to in the spiritual sense. Once we have learnt and experienced a particular situation and dealt with it with love and empathy, we don't need that experience again. It is when we do not learn the lesson that we experience the same situations, in slightly different scenarios, time and time again. The more we embrace life and let go of the old and the negative the better and the more positive our lives will become.

Michael Newton's two books, *Journey of Souls* and *Destiny of Souls* are both excellent reading and can help in understanding more about how this works.

Chapter 3:   Spirit Release

A couple of years after I started doing past life regression, I was introduced to spirit release work. One of the things that I had found difficult to understand was that people often went into past lives that to me didn't feel right. I couldn't explain it at the time and, although the lives they were seeing were perfectly plausible, somehow I wasn't convinced that they belonged to the person who was 'seeing' them.

Once I discovered spirit release work I began to get answers. I attended a course on this subject in London, with an amazing Australian psychic and teacher called Lucy Baker (www.lucybaker. net). Everything she taught me has been invaluable in my work so I am very grateful to her. She explained how we often pick up spirit attachments. In a way, this is no different to picking up a virus or a fungal infection. These wayward spirits are attracted to what is negative about us. So what exactly is a spirit attachment?

Spirit attachments

The main part of our soul always stays in the spirit world. The part of us that is born as a particular person into a particular lifetime is not all of who we are. Normally at the end of a lifetime the dead person, let's call him Fred, sees a white light. Fred follows that light until he finds himself in the spirit world where he receives healing and recovers from the traumas of the lifetime he has just experienced. He is also reunited with the main part of his soul. If, however, Fred does not feel worthy of going back to the light, the fragment of his soul that is Fred stays earthbound and hangs around.

Let us say, for example, that Fred spent a lot of time beating his wife and gambling away his earnings. When he dies he is afraid that he will go to Hell, or at the very least he will be punished by God.

He finds himself out of his body and thinks it may be safer to stay where he is rather than have to face the punishment he knows he deserves. He completely ignores the white light and, when he later decides to look for it, it is gone so he is stuck. There is no such thing as time in the spirit world so he remains where he is, or he may find himself drifting towards one of his old haunts. His lust for gambling is still there so he attaches himself to someone who has the same love of gambling. This way he can still feel the kick of what it is like to gamble. He also feels as though he has a body again and sometimes actually begins to believe that this is his body. He may or may not understand that it is not him actually doing the gambling, but he can still feel the thrill through the other body, so he sends psychic messages to the person to encourage them to gamble even more.

The person who he is attached to is not aware of Fred's presence, but does feel the urge to gamble even more and doesn't know why. Fred will then stay with that gambler for the rest of the gambler's life and then move on to another body when the gambler passes over.

Sometimes spirits hang around because they feel that they are being helpful to a specific person. For example, a deceased mother may hang around her child because she has made a vow to never leave them. These vows need to be broken and the spirit moved to the light because any spirit attachment, even one who thinks they are helping, always takes energy from the person who is living.

Other earth bound spirits don't feel they can leave because they are very angry about something. Their anger and their vows of vengeance are tying them to the earth plane.

Another example could be a woman who has experienced a miscarriage or is mourning the loss of a stillborn baby. If she is still very upset about her loss she may be psychically open and may well pick up a spirit attachment who could be a woman that has also suffered a similar loss.

Sometimes when we die we may feel the need to stay earthbound through a sense of guilt, anger or loss. When this happens a fragment, or the personality we were, stays earthbound. This creates a wayward spirit who is in effect lost and may well attach itself to someone else with whom it resonates. These fragments always attach themselves to the negative traits in a person. So, in the case of the woman who has lost her baby, the soul fragment will make her feel even worse.

Some people can have spirit attachments with them for the whole of their life and never know it. Someone else may suddenly feel very strange and negative without knowing why. Spirit attachments, or entities as they are sometimes called, are always detrimental because they are parasites taking the energy of the living person.

Sometimes these entities are with us for many different lifetimes; tied to us though oaths and vows of love or vengeance.

Drinkers, drug addicts and smokers are notorious for picking up spirit attachments. This is because many wayward spirits still want to feel what it is like to smoke and drink. The client will often hear what they believe is their own inner voice encouraging them to smoke or drink more. I have been in pubs with a very clairvoyant friend of mine who sees wayward spirits attach themselves to people who are particularly susceptible. The drunker someone gets, the more open they are to negative energies and the more those negative energies make the person want to carry on drinking. So it all becomes a vicious circle and one of the reasons why people who abuse alcohol find it so hard to stop drinking.

This explanation may sound weird and rather far-fetched to someone who considers themselves normal and very rational. Nevertheless if someone does have a bad and very negative spirit attached to them, they will instantly feel better the moment it is removed.

My clairvoyant friend also sees spirit attachments on people as he walks down the street. He will often say: "Wow, did you see that one on him?" Of course my answer is always no, because even though I am fairly clairaudient (hear spirit voices) and clairseeing (visualising a picture in your head, rather than in front of you) when I do mediumship work, I do not have his wonderful gift of seeing these things in 3D.

I remember from personal experience when I picked up the spirit attachment of an old man. I had attended a crystal healing workshop but left early because I didn't feel the teacher really knew what she was doing. She kept talking about entities and saying she was taking them out of people whilst wildly moving her pendulum about. Unfortunately at the time I didn't have the knowledge to question her, but I just kept feeling more and more uncomfortable as the day went on. I now realise she was indeed removing them from people with her crystals, but she did not know how to send them to the light, so they left the person she was working on and just went straight into the next person. I have since learnt to leave if, for any reason, I feel uncomfortable when I am on a course.

As I left the class I began to feel ill at ease and as I sat in my car I had this overwhelming urge to smoke a cigarette. Now, this was definitely strange as the only time I had ever smoked a few cigarettes was as an eighteen year old dancer trying to look older and more sophisticated than I actually was. This was not me!

I began to feel panicky and not a little unnerved. I was also over an hour's drive away from my home and feeling desperate for a cigarette. On my way home I remembered a psychic friend of mine so I immediately drove to her house. She took one look at me and burst out laughing whilst asking me where I had picked him up from. She described him as an old man with a hat who chain-smoked. She then quickly sent him on his way. I immediately felt better but it was a very strange experience. It also taught me to never open myself up on so-called psychic workshops unless I trust the teacher and know what I am doing.

Some spirits do not know they are dead and are convinced that they are still in their own body. It can be quite amusing when, for example, you have a case of a man who is convinced that it is 1863 and that he is alive and big and strong, when he is actually a wayward spirit in the body of a five foot two inch woman. The spirit can get quite cross and argumentative when you try to tell him otherwise.

I now rarely do past life work without clearing out the wayward spirits first. The way I see it is that even if a client comes to me just out of curiosity to experience past lives, I still owe it to that client to help them to get the most they possibly can out of the experience. Therefore, it is important that the lifetime they are seeing actually belongs to them and not to something they have picked up along the way.

I have also found that if spirit release work is not done before a past life session, the first lifetime someone goes into will, without fail, be that of a spirit attachment. Their sub-conscious mind knows that it is not part of them so it brings it to the surface to be dealt with first.

I believe that many past life regression therapists continually take their clients into the lives of spirit attachments. This is not a deliberate criticism of other therapists – it is just that if they are not taught how to do spirit release work as part of their training, how will they know to do it? This may be fine for a client who just wants to experience going into a past life, but it certainly will not help them to clear completely any emotional issues they may have.

Some people are so psychically open that they keep picking up spirit attachments so it is important to teach them to protect themselves. Dabbling in things like the Ouija board is an easy way to pick up spirit attachments, and a lot of people who sit in circles in churches channel spirit attachments without being aware of what they are doing.

I remember when I first sat in a circle in a spiritualist church; one woman constantly channelled this rather ignorant Irish spirit called Alfie. I didn't understand any more than she did at the time but I now comprehend that she was actually giving voice to the same spirit attachment time and time again. He needed to be released and sent on his way: not given a voice once a week during a spiritualist circle.

What children often see as imaginary friends are in fact wayward spirits. When the child grows up these spirits can stay with them for life unless they are found and sent to the light.

Also a surviving twin may sometimes have the spirit of the dead twin with them. The dead twin can be angry that the first twin got the body and can make their life quite unsettling. The first twin can also have the sense that there is something missing from their life: they don't know what it is until they realise they were meant to be a twin.

The advantage of the client being in hypnosis, when we work with spirit release, is that the client always knows if the perceived spirit attachment is a part of their own personality or something external. Therefore there is never any fear that we are getting rid of a soul fragment belonging to the client. I wasn't actually taught to use hypnosis for spirit release: I just find it easier to work this way both for the client and myself to understand exactly what is going on, and for the client to remember it. My guides always tell me when I am dealing with a spirit attachment and they never let me down.

Releasing oaths and vows

When a spirit has been with a client over a number of lifetimes we need to release all the oaths and vows between the client and the spirit attachment. This frees up the spirit so it can at last go to the light. Anger, vengeance, curses and love can tie spirits together forever; therefore it is important to release these ties so that both the living and the dead spirits can be free.

I have worked with cases where a spirit attachment has created havoc within a marriage. In one case, the spirit was married to a client in another lifetime. They would probably have made vows together to love one another for all eternity. The client was happily living his life unaware of this spirit. The spirit, however, was all too aware of the vows between them and as far as she was concerned her husband was married to someone else.

Every time the client was ready to make love to his wife something would stop it happening. He would just feel they couldn't do it. Deep unexplained feelings of anger, guilt and resentment would surface for no apparent reason, and the new wife would be left feeling totally bemused and rejected. This would lead to the husband and wife having a row and becoming very frustrated with one another: which is of course exactly what the spirit attachment wanted. Once the oaths and vows between the client and the spirit were rescinded and the spirit sent away to the light, the problems within the marriage ceased immediately.

This may sound far fetched but, believe me, it happens. Sometimes women and men come to see me because they just can't seem to find a partner in this lifetime. In those cases we always find oaths and vows from other lives where they have sworn to only love a specific person. The client's loved one may not have been born in this lifetime, and if they are still hanging around in the form of a spirit attachment this is all the more reason for the client not to find love. In these cases again the oaths and vows need to be rescinded and the spirit sent to the light. The client is then completely free to form a new relationship.

Spirit attachments can cause all sorts of pain and all sorts of negative emotions. I remember reading an interesting article by Dr Edith Fiore: one of the pioneers of spirit release and writer of the book *The Unquiet Dead*. In the article she talks about a man who was sent to her because he wanted to cross-dress all the time. Once she had removed a rather dominant female spirit attachment from him he no longer felt any urge to wear a dress, and his cross-dressing habit stopped completely.

Remember my spirit attachment who wanted to smoke? I sometimes work with a GP in Ireland helping his patients not only with depression, panic attacks, etc. but also to stop smoking. I always do spirit release when I work with people who want to stop smoking because, even though the patient may wish to stop smoking, any spirit attachment with them may certainly not want to.

Damaged auras

Spirit attachments can make depressed people feel ten times worse and it can easily become a vicious circle. If antidepressants don't seem to be working doctors often simply increase the dose, which in turn damages the patient's aura even further. People who can see auras very often comment on the difference between people who are on medication and those who aren't. Medication appears to damage an aura, and once it has been damaged this attracts more spirit attachments as the person is more vulnerable.

Sometimes spirit attachments go to people who they know will be able to help them. When I conduct a spirit release session I always seal the room with white light, or else more lost souls will come in.

I usually ask before I do this if there is anyone around who is ready to go to the light. If I feel that there is, I collect them and send them to the light. Then I can seal the room.

It is really important to understand that these lost fragments mean no harm. They are lost and frightened and often really believe they are helping the person they are with. They need to be shown love and compassion. I am afraid I get really angry with those TV programmes made to scare people, as they often open the audience up to negative energies.

Those programmes about exorcism don't help either, because the priest just seems to remove them from one person so they can go straight into someone else. What is the point of that? Spirits hang around because they really don't know where to go. They are lost and they need help. They should not be used to frighten people because that will only make the spirit more scared than it already is. More understanding and empathy is needed so that we can all appreciate how these lost souls need help. They only become aggressive when they feel threatened by people who scare them. They just mirror back people's fear.

I believe that regular spirit release healing teams should go into places such as hospitals and nursing homes. When a patient dies in hospital they often find themselves out of their body and unaware they are dead: because they don't understand this they tend to hang around in the hospital. At the same time, when a person is given a general anaesthetic in hospital, the essence of that person often leaves their body for the duration of the operation. This essentially leaves an empty space for wayward spirits to jump into. Hospitals are breeding grounds for negative energies and I avoid them whenever I can, unless I am asked to go in to clear up something.

Nursing and old peoples homes are other places full of wayward spirits. A few years ago a young girl, let us call her Amanda, came to see me. She worked as a care person in a home for elderly people suffering from Alzheimer's disease. Amanda liked her job but told me that the longer she worked in the home the less energy she had; she was almost feeling that she just couldn't go on because she felt so exhausted. She was very thin and had dark circles under her eyes and really didn't look very well at all. I asked her if she ate normally, and she told me she did. I also asked her about the dark circles under her eyes. Dark circles are immediate signs to me of spirit attachments and Amanda confirmed what I was already thinking; that the dark circles had become much worse since she began working in the home.

I knew where the home was and remembered reading of a case in the newspaper where an elderly man in his nineties had murdered another of the inmates – an elderly woman in her eighties. At Amanda's request I went to the home and found all the energies there to be extremely heavy. As I am not clairvoyant, I could not actually see what was there but I could feel it. All was definitely not well.

I suggested that whilst I was doing spirit release with her, I could also use her as a surrogate to clear out whatever was in the home. She readily agreed because she wanted a clear healthy working environment. Both she and her boss told me that, since the homicide, people would only stay in the murder room for very short periods of time. The room now belonged to a man who they would find, every morning, asleep in the downstairs sitting room. He wasn't aware that a murder had been committed in his room, but kept saying that he would wake up feeling frightened and couldn't sleep there. Something obviously needed to be done for him as well as my client.

When I put Amanda into hypnosis I found that she was absolutely riddled with spirit attachments. Since she had worked in the home she had obviously become a sponge for all the negative energies hanging around there. We brought in the angels and spirit guides and sent them all on their way. Her whole energy changed, the black bags underneath her eyes started to lift and she immediately began to feel better.

Amanda was still more than happy for us to clear out the old peoples home so I put her back into hypnosis and we systematically began to 'walk' mentally through the building.

What I found so interesting about this case is that Amanda recognised a lot of the spirits that were hanging around. She would say something like: "Oh, there is old Alice. She died about six months ago," or "Oh, there's George. He passed shortly after I came to work here."

As most of the patients in the home were Alzheimer sufferers they must have remained confused as to what was going on and where they were, even after they had died. We carefully worked through all the rooms in the house getting all of these lost souls collected and moved to the light before we attempted to go into the room where the murder was committed. I wanted to do this last to make sure that we cleared it completely.

When I asked Amanda to 'walk' into the murder room, the first thing she said was that the room was so dark she was unable to see anything at all. This of course explained everyone's reluctance to stay for any length of time in that room. Everyone is psychic to a certain degree, and unwittingly people were tuning into all the negative energies in that room.

I knew that the spirit of the murdered woman was still in the room so the first thing we did was to bring in the angels and spirit guides to explain to her that she was dead, but she was now safe. We then asked that all the negative energy left in the room be completely cleared and the room be cleansed and transformed by a healing light. This then enabled the lost soul to be led into the spirit world.

To me this case was particularly interesting as it allowed me to see exactly what was going on in the home, and to understand how important it is to help these lost soul fragments that are still earth bound.

Amanda phoned me a few days later to say she was feeling 100% better. She told me the home felt completely different, and the man who had refused to sleep in the murder room was now happy to stay and sleep there all through the night. Quite a result! I was very pleased for them all.

Often a soul fragment belongs to a person who is now living in a different body. I always get it collected and sent to where it needs to go. I trust that whatever then happens is for the soul's greater good.

When I do past life work I frequently find that the lifetime the client chooses to go into is one where a part of them is still earthbound. This soul fragment has gone astray and is lost on the earth plane, rather than either being at peace in the spirit world or fully integrated with the individual as they are now.

The reason this happens is that when someone dies they are often still holding on to many mixed emotions. Fear, anger, vengeance, revenge, and guilt can all give the person the sensation that they are unworthy of going to the light. Also a need may be felt to hang around a particular person or place. Even a fear of going to Hell can influence whether a soul fragment moves on or not. These fragments are what some people see as ghosts.

Phobias

The client's subconscious mind fully understands this situation, which is why it usually tries to try to resolve the most important issues the moment past life work is initiated. It is also the reason why, when someone is suffering from a particularly bad phobia, I usually take them into a past life. This enables them to find and to understand the reason for their fear. A part of them is usually still there hanging around wherever the incident happened. This fragment will be feeling a deep sense of pain and emotion. Therefore it is very important to help the person to release all the old negative emotions so they can completely let the phobia go. The segment is then moved to the light and all the necessary healing and forgiveness is done. The client is then given the choice as to whether the soul fragment needs to stay in the light with the higher self, or be reintegrated with who they are in this lifetime. The person always knows what the best thing is for them and for the fragment, so I have learnt to trust completely the choice of each individual.

This way whatever was causing the client anxiety in this lifetime is at last dispelled. If it doesn't clear immediately more than one lifetime is involved, so the therapist just has to do a bit more work until all the causes of the problem are finally gone. This way of working is a sure-fire way of making sure the problem will never return.

Chapter 4:   Soul Retrieval

It is often not understood how important soul retrieval is. We are always losing bits of ourselves through trauma and we don't have to be dead to do it. For example, if a child is abused the event is so traumatic that the child's soul experiences loss: a part breaks off or fragments. Rather than stay in the body and experience the suffering, that part of the child just leaves and gets lost in another dimension. On some level it is still attached to the child's auric field, but it is completely disassociated from the normal personality of the child. This soul fragment does not grow up with the child but remains traumatised out in the ether. This is why so many people feel that they may have been abused, but can no longer remember the incident unless put into hypnosis and the soul part retrieved.

Different people do this work in different ways. Shamans for example do a lot of soul retrieval work by 'travelling' to find lost soul parts in order to bring them back to the individual.

A traditional shaman is a kind of medicine man or woman traditionally from an indigenous tribe or culture. The word 'shaman' actually originated from the Tungus tribe in Siberia and it means 'one who sees in the dark'. Many people are now beginning to recognise that it is the indigenous people of this world who hold the real key to ancient spiritual knowledge and truth. Through the ages they have passed down the knowledge of how our DNA actually functions within multidimensional levels.

Shamans do not practise within any religious context; they are usually taught from a very early age by another shaman, or their own spirit guides, how to connect with other dimensions and realities. The places they learn to journey to are usually only accessible to us while we are in the dream state.

The shaman sees illness as a spiritual problem caused by soul loss. If the soul completely leaves the body the patient dies. Therefore the shaman knows that by going into an altered state of consciousness, and by travelling into other dimensions, he can find and retrieve the lost soul fragment. Thus bringing back balance and harmony to the individual concerned.

Sandra Ingerman's book, *Soul Retrieval - mending the fragmented self,* makes very good reading for anyone who wants to learn more about shamanic practices.

Hypnosis is also an excellent way to practise soul retrieval as the client, whilst in a hypnotic trance, is able to find and access the lost parts of his or her self.

My way is to take my client into a safe place before we do any work at all. I also tell them if, at anytime during the session, they want to go to their safe place all they have to do is lift their right arm and they will be there. To be honest they never need to do this, but should they see anything they don't like they can instantly leave it behind. I also demonstrate how this works with them.

Clearing trauma and pain

After working with, and clearing out, all of the trauma and pain connected with abuse I tell the client, towards the end of the session, that we are going to find their lost soul fragments and invite them to come back to a safe place. I explain that some of them may be hiding and some may need some persuasion, but now that all the forgiveness is done we can bring them back. I ask the angels and spirit guides to cleanse all of these soul fragments and then I get the client to invite them to come back in through their heart Chakra (Chakras are covered in more detail in Chapter 15).

What is interesting about this exercise is that the client will say things like: "Oh, there is me at three years old when such and such happened and there is me the last time it happened." There are often hundreds of soul fragments, some more ready to come back than others. What is important to remember is that these soul fragments are still the same age and in the same time frame as when they were abused. They are usually traumatised so it is important that they now feel it is safe to come back and stay, or they will just break off again. The client needs to reassure these parts of them that once they are back the abuse will never happen again.

This is powerful work and often a very emotional event for the person experiencing it. Clients often say that after this treatment they feel like a complete person again.

When I work with children and adults who have suffered abuse both in this lifetime and in other lifetimes, forgiveness is always the key. This is usually a very hard thing for the client to do because all abuse victims are extremely angry with their aggressors, but once they can bring themselves to forgive they will feel totally different and emotionally liberated.

I worked with a lady in her sixties who had been severely abused as a child. She was in counselling for more than thirty years but was still furious with the man who abused her. She was locked into her anger. After the first session she was feeling a lot better and by the second she told me she felt entirely different. She was amazed that at last she felt ready to leave the past behind her and to get on with her life. After we brought back many abused and frightened children she said she felt whole for the first time in her life.

Double disassociation

When I work with people who have been abused I usually use a combination of techniques. If the thought of reliving the experience is particularly traumatic, which of course it usually is, I use the NLP method of double disassociation. The client can either watch the whole thing on an imaginary TV screen or watch the scene in an imaginary cinema either from a single (in the auditorium), or doubly (as the projectionist) disassociated point of view. This allows the client to see what is happening without becoming too traumatised.

I don't let the client go as far as reliving the abuse. The inner child method of working is by far the safest and best as far as I am concerned. I tell the client (let us call her Mary) to watch the child on the screen. I don't call the child by her name because I am keeping Mary disassociated from what is happening. Therefore the younger version of herself is always the child. I explain to Mary that we are going to watch the scene, but before any of the abuse happens she is going to jump into the picture and stand in front of the child to protect her and to stop it happening. I explain to Mary that as she is the child's protector she can tell this man whatever she likes, and she can push him away if she wants to, because she is now in charge and the child's defender.

This is an opportunity for Mary to say what she has always wanted to say to her abuser, face to face. It is a chance for her to let out all the years of pent-up anger and frustration she feels towards him, and ultimately towards herself. She may want to push and kick the abuser or she may just want to tell him what she really thinks of him. I just let her do whatever she feels she needs to do. This is when all of those locked up emotions come up and tears start to flow. Remember this is not a process to rush in any way. All of the anger, pain and resentment needs to come up and out. She has suppressed her feelings for all of her adult life so she now needs to feel safe to release all of this anger. This is a new experience for her. She often lets out her pent-up anger and frustrations with the people she loves but she has never, as an adult, come face to face with her abuser before. This work may leave her exhausted, but it will also put her in a place where she can forgive.

Once all of this is done it is time for her to forgive both her abuser and herself for letting it happen. It is also the time to ask the abuser for forgiveness for all of the negative oaths, vows and curses she has continually sent out to him over the years.

This can, however, also be the time when clients go spontaneously into a past life and find the key to everything that has happened. If this doesn't happen, I will often instigate it, especially if I feel that it will clear up stuff on an even deeper level.

Some are ready to forgive and let go, others say things such as: "I know I should forgive him but I just can't." My answer to this is: "All right, but do you think you can forgive yourself for having let it happen?" Logically, clients know that at whatever age they were when the abuse happened, they could never have stopped it. However if we create everything that happens in our lives through our belief systems, clients feel on a deeper level responsible for it having happened. Therefore if we do not forgive ourselves for whatever happens to us, we will never be free of the scenario.

Sometimes clients find it very difficult to forgive themselves, but with a bit of gentle persuasion they will do it. I always say that it is their choice if they forgive themselves. It is not for me to force them to do something they are not one hundred per cent happy with. This enables them to reach a logical conclusion, and they say things such as: "I should forgive myself, shouldn't I?" or "I was a child. It wasn't my fault was it, so why shouldn't I forgive myself?" And so on.

As I mentioned before forgiveness is the key to all of this, so once they have forgiven themselves they are now ready to forgive their abuser. When all of this work is done with the client in deep hypnosis, it is much more powerful. They will very often see their abuser crying and thanking them for finally forgiving them. I also ask the abused to ask their abuser to forgive them for all of the negative thoughts and energy they have been sending out in connection with everything that happened. This always makes forgiveness a three way process, forgiveness of the person who hurt the child, forgiveness from the person who did the abusing and forgiveness of self.

When all of this work is finished, the traumatised soul fragments can be healed and brought back because now they know they are safe. In a case such as Mary's, I would get her to turn around, tell the child she was safe and then pick her up. She can then reintegrate the child within herself. From there she can go into her safe place and find all the other lost child parts of herself.

Since abuse rarely happens just once, this process may need to be repeated a few times in more than one session. It can sometimes be sorted in just one session depending on how ready the client is to let go and to heal themselves.

Dealing with abuse by a parent is invariably the most difficult because they are the people we should be able to trust completely in this world. However, this work is always very powerful and it really allows the client to start to feel free probably for the first time in their life.

Parental issues come up again and again and usually take the most working through. We choose our parents and often they are the people we need to sort out the most with.

Soul groups

We are all part of soul groups, and the members of our soul groups are usually the people we incarnate with again and again. It is with these souls that we learn our most difficult lessons. In the spirit world we trust these souls implicitly, so when we want to experience something difficult or traumatic we choose them to teach us.

Difficult experiences help us to grow. So, what may seem to us to be a very challenging period in our life is often the moment we become truly free. These times force us to make decisions, they make us take action and they stop us being complacent. These lessons teach us to become more at one with who we truly are, and they help us to understand what we should really be doing in order to become a happy, stronger, more balanced individual.

Chapter 5:   Oaths and Vows

During past life work we often meet other souls who we have ill-treated and who have wronged us in other lifetimes. This is not necessarily abuse. It can be in battles, domestic violence, robbery etc. Until we forgive them and they forgive us, we meet them time and time again to give us an opportunity to sort out our differences and to be free. Our thoughts create who we are so we need to let go of all feelings of anger and vengeance, because by holding on to these things we are actually only hurting ourselves. We owe it to ourselves to rescind all oaths and vows we have made with both our enemies and our loved ones in any lifetime or in any dimension. We also need to withdraw any curses and make sure they are resolved and dissolved for ever.

Belief systems

The word 'curse' can bring up many feelings, but again it is about belief. If you believe you are sending out a curse to someone, and that person believes they are cursed by you, then that is what will happen. If curses don't exist deeply within your belief system, how can they hurt you? It is important to understand that you will not be affected by what someone is saying about you if, at the very core of your being, you do not believe it to be true. However people continually mirror our beliefs, so if something like that comes into your life there may be a part of you that on a deeper level accepts it. It is happening because you need to find and to clear up the cause.

People often ask me questions such as: "If I rescind the vows I made with my husband in other lifetimes, does this mean he will then leave me in this?" I tell them of course not; it will probably bring them closer together because they will be with one another through choice, rather than locked into something they don't fully comprehend.

It is not generally understood how important it is to release all the old oaths and vows from every lifetime. People make oaths, vows, promises and verbal contracts all the time, but what is not usually known is how binding these are, and how they create etheric ties forever unless they are retracted and dissolved back into the light.

We make hundreds of vows in many different lifetimes. The vows to the church are usually the most powerful and often the most damaging. Vows of chastity, poverty, silence, to renounce all other faiths and absolute obedience are just a few. The power of the Catholic Church never fails to amaze me, and also how many people go back into lifetimes where they were nuns, monks and priests. All of these vows are still standing, together with the vows we have made within a church service to love someone for all eternity, and perhaps to always be obedient to a husband if it was a woman marrying a man.

The oath of poverty

The list just goes on and on. All of this stuff may have happened centuries ago, but remember time isn't linear and these ties are still binding until released. How can anyone enjoy a happy sexual relationship with their new partner when, on a far deeper level, they know they are a bride of Christ with a vow of chastity to remain pure only to him for all eternity?

Healers often have great problems with taking money for their work. They know they are offering a service and they realise they need to live and pay their bills. They also recognise that people have free

31

will as to whether to use their services. The oath of poverty is always there, together with all the old beliefs about it not being right to take money for healing people. Yet often there is deep conflict and guilt that is difficult for them to let go of. It appears to be quite rare to have experienced just one life within the church. When I work with a client and find a lifetime as a nun, monk or a priest, I always expect to find more. I also wait for deep feelings of guilt about everything to surface. Once all of this is cleared the client feels much freer and able to move forward.

These vows are always detrimental because they stop us fulfilling ourselves and arriving at our full potential. Once these oaths and vows are released, there is often profound change.

Over the years, I have regressed many people who are working as healers in this lifetime. I always find hypnosis interesting with these people because they usually mirror back to me my own unresolved issues, in a way that is often very obvious to me.

One of the problems I had to resolve when I began this occupation was expecting the client to pay me for my efforts. I was giving people my time and I was doing my utmost to help them to heal themselves, but I felt that what I was doing should be given for free. The strange thing was that up until that time whether I was dancing, interpreting or selling I would always expect to be paid for whatever my employment was. Why was I in some way judging healing differently? Of course my logical mind knew that if I was going to work full time in the healing business I needed to graciously receive payment for my services. My subconscious however was appalled at this prospect.

Many healers have this problem and nine out of ten times it relates to vows of poverty and obedience they made to the Catholic Church in other lifetimes. Healers and therapists have often been nuns, monks, priests etc. Unfortunately all of these pledges are still standing unless the individual chooses to renounce them. Once these promises are let go, the person is set free and understands that it is reasonable to charge for their services.

Rescinding these vows will also help to break the pattern of attracting clients who hold the belief that any healing they receive should be free of charge. It is important to remember how people judge the worth of something by what it costs. Therefore, if healers give away their services for free, their work can sometimes be considered of little or no value by the prospective client. Medical practitioners frequently charge exorbitant amounts in their practices, so why shouldn't alternative practitioners, who have also spent thousands of pounds, and many years studying, receive remuneration for what they do?

The other issue many of these people have is the deep rooted fear that if they do their chosen work they will suffer or be punished in some way. Time and time again when I work with healers they go back to the witch hunts, where they find themselves trying to run and hide from the Inquisition. Or they see themselves being burned at the stake. These men and women were usually just the equivalent of the local medicine person who gathered herbs and poultices to help heal the sick. Or perhaps they were just women who having experienced childbirth themselves fell into the role of midwife just to help others. They were however considered a huge threat to the church, so much so that they were captured, tortured and burned.

Their experiences have left many people with deeply rooted fears. I was one such person. So much so that I almost attracted the same burning experience to myself in this lifetime, although when it happened in 1988 I had none of the understanding I now have.

When I was living in Calabria in southern Italy I owned a fast food restaurant with my then partner. It was very near the sea and because we had no mains gas we used bottled LPG. These large gas bottles were kept in a locked cupboard on the outside of the building. A pipe then carried the gas underneath the restaurant floor and up into the kitchen.

It was unusually cold for that time of year and I was feeling feverish because I was suffering from bronchitis. At the time I was really too ill to be there, but the lady who worked in the kitchen was in hospital. She had just undergone a serious thyroid operation so I really had no choice but to get on with it.

Doing what I always did, I opened up one of the heavy metal shutters to allow me access to the restaurant. I knew my partner would pull up the other shutters when he stopped talking to his brother who lived upstairs. I went into the kitchen to light the griddle plate so that it would be hot and ready for use when we opened the other doors.

Of course, because I was suffering from bronchitis, I couldn't smell anything so I didn't smell the gas that had been slowly leaking into the kitchen for the past twelve hours. I opened up the hotplate and lit the match. Whoosh, the flame shot out of the hotplate, around my head and left shoulder and then circled my body before going out of the kitchen and into the main bulk of the restaurant. There was then a loud bang as the three remaining metal shutters and doors blew out. My handbag blew off my shoulder: it was later found by the greengrocer in his courtyard next door.

I remember just standing there, as at the time I didn't seem to know what else to do. My partner appeared from upstairs and started yelling at me to get out of the kitchen, which I did. My hair was alight and my trousers were ablaze up to my knees. Luckily because it was so cold I was still wearing a thick padded jacket and it probably saved my life. I still remember the old, very polite, greengrocer from next door asking me if he had my permission to pat my legs so that he could put the flames out. I don't remember who extinguished my flaming hair- probably my partner.

Somehow I didn't die. The walls of the kitchen must have protected me, but I am sure that had I been in the main body of the restaurant I would have exploded in the same way as the doors did. My partner's life was saved because he was upstairs with his brother.

I was in hospital for about ten days and then spent another two weeks at home. I will always be grateful for the treatment and the care I received in that little hospital high up in Belvedere in Calabria. The doctors and nurses were amazing, and if I have little or no scar tissue it is totally down to them. My face, hands and feet were covered in second degree burns and all of these swelled up to at least double their normal size. I looked like a monster. So much so that when some of my staff came to visit me they walked straight past the bed and didn't recognise me at all.

When, many years later, I asked my guides to show me what all this was about I was told that my partner was the one who had burned me in the Inquisition. I paid him back by making him face the consequences of what he had done. Interestingly, he was certainly more in shock with what had happened than I was. I enjoyed lovely treatment and a complete rest: while he had to bear the sight of my injuries and sort out all the problems the explosion caused to the restaurant.

I hope I have now let all of that go, and that I have forgiven all of my lifetimes that were in any way connected with the Inquisition.

Vows of love

We have also made oaths and vows to love a particular soul forever. Now that is all well and good providing the two of you are free to be together in this lifetime, but what if you are not? Or what if the person you have vowed to love forever is not even born into this lifetime, or is of a completely different generation or sex. Remember sometimes we have lives as men, and in others we have lives as women so all of this can get pretty complicated.

I frequently have people come to me who say they are unable to form solid relationships. Some just don't know why this is, and others say things such as: "I know there is someone out there for me, but I just can't seem to find him or her."

When I take these people into past lives we always find oaths and vows to love a particular soul forever; to the exclusion of all others. This is very binding and is stopping the person finding someone they can truly love in this lifetime.

Remember we have experienced thousands of different lifetimes, and made vows again and again to different souls, so we have numerous etheric ties with countless people. These may be vows of love, but they may equally be vows of anger, hatred and revenge.

We may have strong etheric love ties with more than one person and they may happen to be around in this lifetime. This can cause enormous complications, especially if the person believes they love both souls equally.

Of course not all vows are about love. Vows of vengeance are equally powerful because those involved will reappear again and again in every lifetime, unless the vows are rescinded and everyone is forgiven.

Vengeance is often a two-way thing to be sorted between two people. This is fine if the two people come in as a couple, but that doesn't happen very often. Everyone has a higher self, a part of us that never leaves the spirit world and so always understands the bigger picture. During hypnosis it is possible for the client to bring in the higher self of the other person so that all of the oaths, vows, etc. can be resolved and dissolved between them and forgiveness can finally allow all of these issues to be put to rest. It is amazing how relationships can change for the better once this work has been done.

People often come to see me and tell me they want to divorce their partner. They tell me that they have been separated for years but keep coming back together, or they don't want to be with the other person anymore, but it is as if there is an invisible cord keeping them together. Once the oaths and vows are rescinded and the ties cut, they are suddenly free to pursue their lives as individuals.

Promises can be equally damaging. For example, if you promise to be around for your children forever, you may well find yourself old and infirm in an old people's home desperately hanging on, probably with diminished mental faculties, but at the same time unable to leave the earth plane. This may seem a bit far fetched but it is important to understand what we are doing when we make oaths and vows to people.

Oaths of allegiance

We swear allegiances to countries and to various leaders. This often helps us to understand why sometimes we feel so much more at home in a country that is not the actual country of our birth, and also why we sometimes have a strong affinity with a certain historical period. When we return to places where we have experienced past lives we often have strong feelings of recognition of these areas. Logically, in this life, we know it is the first time we have visited somewhere, but we also know that we are familiar with where we are.

The first time I visited Italy I felt instantly as if I had come home. I also found the language incredibly easy to learn. Since then I have visited many of my own past lives, and most of the ones I have seen have taken place in Italy. This explains why, in many respects, Italy feels more like my country than England ever has. Yet at the same time I feel completely English so I am a rather odd combination. I probably promised allegiance to both countries in more than one lifetime.

Interestingly, until a few years ago, I was travelling to Italy about once a month, but since I have cut many of my ties with the country and released all my oaths and vows to it, I don't feel the need to keep going back. Our subconscious mind never forgets anything but it does allow us to release old oaths, vows and promises so that we are free to move on.

Our subconscious minds also retain foreign languages and people can often understand these when they are under hypnosis, although they may not be able to speak them. I had a fascinating experience working with a young girl who was about eighteen years old. Whilst in hypnosis she started speaking to me in fluent French. When I brought her back she completely remembered the experience, but she was no longer able to understand French. She had also failed her French exam at school.

She later told me that when she listened to a recording of herself afterwards she was unable to understand what she had been saying, and had to ask someone who spoke French to translate it for her! Working with the subconscious is so fascinating because it allows us to access parts of ourselves of which we are unaware.

Chapter 6:   Inside the Womb and Healing Physical and Emotional pain

We know so much more about ourselves and about other people than we realise. A very powerful way of working is to use hypnosis to take someone back into the womb. It always amazes me how the foetus is still so connected to the spirit world whilst knowing what it wants to achieve in this new life. The baby will fully appreciate why its soul has chosen these parents, and at the same time is able to experience all of the mother's thoughts, emotions and everything she is feeling about bringing this new baby into the world.

Clients will often say things such as: "The soul who will be my father in this lifetime is really excited about my being born. We have been together in many lifetimes, and I am coming to help him to learn more about how to love himself and others in this lifetime," or "I have chosen a mother who I love this time around, and I know she will really love me."

Sometimes the mother is really happy about the prospect of having the baby, but at other times it is a really different story. The client will say things such as: "She doesn't want me. She is only having me to please her husband," or "The woman who is to be my mother in this lifetime is really frightened of childbirth; she doesn't want to have to go through it all."

Other times they say: "She wanted to abort me but it was too late," or "She also tried to take pills and things but they didn't work.

She really doesn't want me. I am dreading being born this time around."

Parents-to-be are often afraid that a new baby will take too much love from them, leaving less love and attention for each other. The foetus will then tune into thoughts from both the mother and the father, and know their deepest insecurities and fears.

Choosing your role

Sometimes the client will say things such as: "My mother and I had a really difficult time in the last life when we were sisters, and this time I am coming back to try to resolve the situation between us. It will be difficult because she will recognise me and not like me, but I have to try this time because we need to sort out our differences." These sorts of statements often help the client to gain insight. The person begins to realise that they themselves have chosen this role and how it is up to them to try to improve their relationship with either, or both, parents.

Being born a girl can also be a problem to an incoming soul. People will say things such as: "I am really dreading being born this time around because I am going to be a girl. I would much rather be a boy because boys have a much easier time of it", while others will say "This lifetime is about learning to be more in tune with my feelings and emotions, and being born a girl will give me more opportunity to do this."

Over the years I have worked with many men and women, and have overwhelmingly found that men put their feelings into boxes. As a hypnotist or healer I can deal with this box and their problems will be instantly resolved. Women are much more complex to work with as they allow their emotions to cross over into every aspect of their lives.

This is fascinating stuff because again it allows the person to understand that this is their choice. They are exactly where they need to be. So now they can start to show compassion for themselves and for others in relation to everything that is going on in their lives. Working with the baby in the womb can really improve the way someone feels about themselves now. It can also help them to understand that parents are human and they make mistakes just like the rest of us.

Some hypnotherapists take people back into past lives by taking the client into the womb in this life, and then getting them to travel further back. I don't personally use this method much, but I do often take clients into the womb and into the inter-life where they are planning this new lifetime. This is a good way for the person to remember what it is they are here to achieve this time around.

We have experienced thousands of past lives – most of them probably quite boring and mundane. We have been both men and women living in many different countries, speaking many different languages.

Seeking resolution

The past lives I try to work with are the ones that need to be resolved in some way. So often we lock both emotional and physical pain in our bodies as a result of unresolved issues – usually anger, resentment and guilt. We express anger at other people, but this is really anger at ourselves. Once the situation is seen, understood and resolved by releasing the anger then the pain can go.

This work is often multilayered and is rather like peeling an onion. The root cause of one specific pain can be found and cleared in just one past life session. Occasionally it may take a little longer. It can be that lifetime after lifetime has compounded the pain by the same scenarios being repeatedly played out in different ways. Clients may then become very angry with certain people and parts of themselves from many different lifetimes.

To clear this, the therapist needs to visit all of the important lifetimes where this anger is being retained, and then to help the client resolve and dissolve it. The less important ones usually drop away once this has been achieved.

One of the methods I use, when working with people in hypnosis, is to tell them that I am throwing a pack of cards into the air. I instruct them to watch the cards, and say that if any of these should land face upwards rather than face downwards, those will be the lifetimes they still need to clear. Sometimes the client will just see one card facing upwards and on other occasions there will be many. I then tell the person to walk into what they feel is the main card.

It really doesn't matter which it is; this is just a means of getting the person's subconscious mind to find the key to the problem. I ask them to 'walk' into that card and look down at their feet, and be back in the lifetime they need to resolve. Once we have done whatever work we need to do there, we can then go back to the rest of the cards. They might then say that all the cards are facing downwards or, if there are still issues to sort out, they will name the next card they want to 'walk' into. We continue to do this until the person sees all the cards facing downwards. This can also be done using doorways or anything else as long as it helps that person to focus their mind.

Another way of working is to ask where the emotion is being held in the body. Of course this is easy to find if it is the source of the person's physical pain, but we also lock unresolved emotions into our body, so in hypnosis a person can just as easily find where they are holding emotional pain. Just think of the language we use about ourselves and other people. "She is a real pain in the neck" or, "I feel really bitter about this relationship, he has broken my heart", etc.

Manifesting emotional problems

We then often manifest these emotional problems into physical illnesses. The lungs hold deep grief, the liver-anger, the gall-bladder bitterness; constipation is about holding on to things that really need to be got rid of. In my experience of working with women with breast cancer, a common factor is that they nurture everyone in their family but themselves. Shoulder pain can be caused by someone feeling that they have the weight of the world on their shoulders, while leg pains can be connected with an inability to move forward, and so it goes on. The language a person uses can often help a therapist to understand what is really going on.

Specific pains in the body are sometimes caused by a past life injury. There may not be any logical explanation as to why a client has a problem with their back or hip, but nevertheless they are in pain. By getting the person to mentally 'walk' into the cause of the pain, and seeing the lifetime it is associated with, this can then be released as follows:

1: Understanding the cause of the problem, for example seeing themselves stabbed by someone;
2: Forgiving whatever caused the injury to happen whether it is a person, an animal or even an inanimate object;
3: Forgiving themselves for allowing it to have happened;
4: Releasing all oaths and vows of vengeance against whom or what caused the incident to happen;
5: Rescinding any curses against the cause and against themselves because it happened;
6: Checking to see if that soul fragment is earth bound and if it needs to be moved on to the light;
7: Checking to see if there are other lifetimes that connect with the pain and, if there are, sorting them out;
8: Cleansing and releasing the physical body of all the memories connected with the injury.

Once all of this has been done the client no longer has a reason to hold on to any of these old memories. It is emotions such as anger, guilt and resentment that caused the person to hold on to the pain. Once these are released so is the pain.

If we often keep on injuring a certain part of our body in this life, this is the soul's way of getting us to look deeply into the root cause of the problem so that it can be released once and for all. Clear up the past life problem and then you are clearing up this life's problems as well.

Chapter 7: Phobias

Working with phobias is one of the most fascinating aspects of my job. Phobias are usually caused by past life problems when a soul fragment is stuck in a particular time, where it keeps reliving a certain incident such as drowning or suffocating in a fire.

I recently helped a young mother called Audrey. She was suffering from emetophobia and was also very afraid that her husband would leave her. Emetophobia is a fear of feeling and being sick. This phobia can sometimes be connected to something that happened when the person was a child. For example, they may have been sick at school and were made fun of by the other pupils, or a parent may not have been around to support them when they were unwell.

Sometimes it can however be a past life problem, as in Audrey's case. She clearly remembered being sick as a child but of being totally supported by her mother so I didn't feel this was the root cause. I took her back and asked her to go through a big doorway with a big key attached to the door. Often by using metaphors, such as the key in the door, the client's subconscious mind will find the solution to the problem.

Audrey went straight back to the time of the black plague in Europe. She was again a young mother whose name was Marianna. Her husband had already died from the illness, leaving her alone to nurse two young children who were also ill with the disease. Marianna did everything she could for them but they both died. The young mother was heartbroken and felt a deep sense of guilt for not being able to save her children. She never contracted the malady but she lived the rest of her life with a deep sense of loss and blame.

At the end of that lifetime she did not go to the light as she was still very much earthbound, and still locked into all of those negative emotions. As I moved her into the light she suddenly became aware of her husband and children holding out their arms to her. Then, because she felt safe at last, she was able to let go and forgive herself for what she saw as her failures in that lifetime. She also understood why she was carrying a fear that her husband would leave her.

People are often afraid of the dark and of closed spaces as a result of lives where they were imprisoned. Men and women who are afraid to speak up or speak out in public, or who don't like feeling ties or tight jewellery around their necks, have often been hanged or strangled in a past life.

Psychic people often run away from their powers because of a deep fear of being accused of witchcraft. In hypnosis they often go back to being burnt at the stake. Many of these women were just healers who used herbs and poultices to cure the sick. It is often the smell of burning they remember the most. Whilst some that suffered those atrocities went off to the light, many still hang around, since they are angry and feel they have been deeply wronged by someone.

Weight problems can be a result of starvation or, in some rare cases, gluttony in other lifetimes. Addictions are often brought forward and can make some people more susceptible to temptation than others. Addictions always improve once the past life trauma is sorted out.

Many illnesses are also related to past life trauma. People attract an illness to them as punishment for something they believe they have done terribly wrong. The HIV virus seems to be a good example of this, as all the people I have worked with who have this illness were suffering from a deep sense of guilt, and felt that they were somehow paying themselves back by contracting the virus.

Asthma is usually connected to smoke inhalation, or some other incident where the person suffocated due to a lack of air.

Childbirth phobias

Phobias and illnesses connected to children and childbirth are common. Women who suffer from problems such as endometriosis and fibroids seem to be cases in point. If a woman has suffered the loss of a child in a previous lifetime, or suffered a grave injustice, these illnesses are often prevalent. It is especially important to work on forgiveness when this comes up, as women will still believe it is their fault and will often develop problems in this life when they reach childbearing age. It will become their way of paying themselves back for whatever they believe they are guilty of. Or there could also be vows of chastity in place, so this is their way of not breaking these vows. Of course, this is all on a deep subconscious level, and the person will have no awareness of any of these things until they are put into deep hypnosis.

Self punishment can also happen in this lifetime. For example, if at a young age a woman becomes pregnant and then decides on an abortion, she may later pay herself back by either continuing to miscarry every time she becomes pregnant, or by creating an illness whereby she cannot conceive again.

Similarly when someone is very afraid of either becoming pregnant, or of actually having a child, there is usually a deep fear of something that happened before recurring again. They may be suffering either deep physical or emotional pain. Once the past life issues are completely cleared the fear disappears and the person can get on with their life.

Phobias can stop us going on holiday or travelling for work. For example, a lady who came to me with a fear of flying: she had recently been in an aeroplane that dropped many feet in the air as it hit an air pocket. People were screaming and shouting, and the whole incident terrified her.

I thought at the time that this incident may be related to a past life, but the client was not ready to go deeper to explore what this could be. We worked on all the fear connected to the incident and she felt a lot better. A few months later she phoned me again to say that, although she had improved, she still had some fear of flying. Now she was ready to go deeper and to explore more by doing past life work.

This time I started working with her using Theta Healing and asking her what would be the worst thing that could happen if the plane crashed. This is a classic way of getting to what is in the subconscious mind without hypnosis. She immediately said to me "I would die and have to leave my husband and child". This was a very interesting answer because, although at the time she was engaged to be married, she had neither a husband nor child.

I took her into hypnosis and asked her to find the lifetime connected to all of this. She went straight back to a time in her last lifetime when she was a passenger on a plane. The plane crashed and she found herself running up and down the aisle. I asked her why she was doing this and she told me she had to get out to see her husband and child because everyone else was dead.

My guides were telling me that she too was dead, so I asked her to walk back to her seat. When we did this at first she didn't understand what she was seeing because she saw herself still strapped into her seat looking dead.

I told her that everything was going to be OK and I was going to bring her guides in so that she could be collected and go to the light. She started to cry because she told me she was not ready to leave her husband and young child behind. I told her they would understand and we would meet them in the light.

Once we took her into the light she was able to talk to the higher self of both her husband and child, and to ask them to forgive her for getting herself killed and for leaving them behind. After she did this she told me everything was now resolved and she could now move on.

I then took her forward in time to her next plane journey. She saw herself happy, travelling thousands of miles and feeling completely safe and relaxed on the aeroplane. The phobia was gone.

Abandoning loved ones

As evidenced, this was not really fear of flying; it was about fear of abandoning loved ones. She is now happy to fly anywhere in the world, and recently she flew to New Zealand for her honeymoon with her new husband – something she could not have even contemplated a few months ago.

I once worked with a lady who had suddenly developed a fear of riding her horse. Jean (as we'll call her,) had ridden since she was a child and being around horses was second nature to her. She had recently fallen off her horse during a club meeting but, as she had fallen off horses many times in the past, she couldn't understand why she had suddenly become so afraid after this particular incident.

Once she was in hypnosis I took her back to the day of the incident, and I suggested that she talk me through everything that happened on that day from the moment she got up. As she began to do this she suddenly burst into tears. I asked her how she was feeling and what was the matter? She told me how she was feeling really sad because she always went to the club event with her friend (let us call her Susan). When I asked her why she wasn't going with Susan this time, she told me that she had recently been killed in a car crash and this was the first time she had to go to the event without her friend. We continued to work through the events of the day until we came to the time when someone hit her horse quite hard on the rump: the horse reared and she fell off.

I asked her if she was physically hurt in any way and she said "no". Apart from being rather angry at the person who had behaved in such an irresponsible way, she was actually fine – although she did say she wasn't sure if she wanted to ride her horse any more. As the fear developed from the time the horse was slapped and she hit the ground, I told her to go back in time again.

This time we took the whole thing into slow motion, and I asked her to explain to me exactly what was going on in her head from the second she started to fall. She immediately said: "If I die now there is no one to look after my son, James." When I asked her why this was suddenly a problem now and why she had not felt like this at other times, she told me that Susan was James's godmother, and she had always promised to look after him if anything ever happened to her. Now that Susan was dead, if she also died, the child would be left alone with no one to look after him.

Once she realised what all this was about she was no longer afraid of riding her horse; she could finally forgive the man and stop blaming the poor animal for her fears.

The causes of phobias can be fascinating to work with from a therapist's point of view. A few years ago a lady who was very phobic about small, dark, confined spaces came to see me. She went back to a life where as a little pauper boy of about seven, she was forced to be a chimney sweep's assistant in 17th century London. The child was constantly pushed up tight, shadowy, dirty flues in order to sweep them. He was made to carry heavy brushes, and felt his toes being pricked by metal rods if he hesitated on his way up. He was absolutely terrified of the dark and every day, and every new chimney, meant a new terror for him.

He died of suffocation when he eventually fell down a flue and ended up covered in soot. Again we had to work on the forgiveness. The little boy was angry at his master for continually forcing him up chimneys, and he was angry at himself for being so powerless. This soul fragment was very angry that it was still hanging around so we took it to the light where it was cleansed and healed. He then felt able to forgive the man who was his master and his soul fragment was able to integrate back with its owner. The phobia was gone and the client felt more whole.

I have worked with many different phobias. People who are afraid of confined spaces have often been trapped somewhere; those who are afraid of water are usually drowned; others afraid of fire have suffocated and so on. Often people who are afraid of standing up in front of other people have been publicly humiliated in some way. The soul fragment is usually stuck somewhere and angry because of what happened to it.

Fear comes in so many guises, but by finding the root cause and eradicating the anger, resentment, pain, guilt and other negative emotions, the phobia can be released. Often phobias are interconnected with quite a few different lifetimes, but as long as the therapist clears the lives that relate to the problem the phobia will never return. All of this does, of course, make my work endlessly fascinating as no two cases are ever the same.

Chapter 8: Reclaiming Our Power

As I mentioned before, past lives connected to the church are very common and often extremely damaging. Oaths made to God, as understood by the Catholic Church, often hold deep psychological implications for the souls who made them. We also often hold God responsible for all the terrible things that happen to us, which we believe are beyond our control.

Church lives are very common, especially when we think of how often women were shut up in nunneries, and how younger sons of affluent families were frequently expected to go into the church. In countries such as Ireland, proud mothers wanted sons to become priests, and women who couldn't find a husband became nuns.

Many of these types of beliefs are locked in our subconscious minds. We continually punish and chastise ourselves for the bad things that happen to us, without understanding that it is these beliefs that are causing them to happen.

Another thing that often happens as a result of these past lives is that people find themselves waking up at certain times during the night. It seems they are still waking up for prayers at whatever time their subconscious mind is telling them to rise.

I had a real problem with this until I renounced all my vows to the Catholic Church. I was not brought up to be a Catholic in this lifetime, but I kept waking up exactly at two and six o'clock every morning. I don't know what these particular times mean, but I have seen lives connected to Rome and the church, so a part of me was obviously still practising some sort of obedience.

Unconditional love

We hold so much guilt in relation to our beliefs about God, and because of this we often believe we are unworthy, unclean and completely unlovable. God could never, ever love us and therefore how can we possibly love ourselves when we are of such little merit? If God is all-seeing, all-loving and all-forgiving why would he (or she) wish us to be unhappy and unfulfilled by keeping us without love, poor and feeling worthless? The way I see it is that the Creator, or God if you like, is all about unconditional love and light therefore we need to stop punishing ourselves and others with our negative beliefs.

As a therapist I work with so many damaged souls, and the more negative beliefs these people hold, the more difficult it is for them to let go and to feel free. It is important to learn how to take total responsibility for ourselves, and our actions, without ever blaming God or other people then we can be totally free and stand in our own power.

From a very young age we are taught to give up our individuality and strength. We put ourselves in the hands of priests, doctors, bank managers, teachers, etc. We accept various ridiculous laws and we tend to believe what politicians tell us. We are constantly bombarded with negativity and newspeak from the media; yet we repeatedly buy newspapers. It seems to me that all news and TV documentaries are based on what terrible thing might happen next. Very little is actual fact, so this just generates more and more fear within the population.

We give our education over to teachers who indoctrinate our offspring with their version of the world. Of course not all teachers are bad. Some are very loving and caring towards the children. However, if these people have negative viewpoints they will implant these ideas into the minds of the very young. They will help to produce children with a limited outlook and restricted belief systems.

Children up to the age of about seven are constantly functioning in the alpha and theta brainwaves, so they absorb all information very quickly into their subconscious minds. This is fine if the information they are given about themselves and others is positive, but what if most of it is negative? These children will very quickly find themselves with harmful core beliefs about themselves and their own ability to function in this world.

Brainwaves

To understand this better we need to know that as adults we spend most of our time functioning in the Beta brainwave measured at 13-40 hertz. This is normal waking consciousness and allows us to solve problems and to reason.

When we day dream we are in alpha brainwave, measured at 7-13 hertz. This is when we are relaxed, possibly thinking and visualising what we want for dinner. Or we are thinking about that great guy or girl we just met. We go into alpha when we watch television, when we learn, or are being creative.

Theta is measured at 4-7 hertz. This is that semi-conscious state between asleep and awake – that dreamlike experience after the alarm clock has sounded and we should be getting up, but we are still experiencing the dream we are in. This is also the brain wave used for deep hypnosis.

Delta is when we are fast asleep and brain waves are measured at less than 4 hertz.

And finally there is gamma at 40+ hertz. This is when the brain is hyper alert but seems to slow down during events such as a car accident. It is also the brainwave that allows a mother to rush out and save her child from an oncoming car.

Some of the world's best healers, such as Vianna Stibal (www. thetahealing.com) and Dr Richard Bartlett (www.matrixenergetics. com), have been found to work in gamma when they perform miraculous healings on people. I have watched Dr Bartlett instantly heal a broken foot. He also completely corrected my round shoulders in a matter of seconds when I attended one of his courses. My back has been straight ever since!

Hypnotherapists work with people in alpha and theta brainwaves. This is because in these waves people are very open to positive (and negative) suggestions. If, for example, someone wants to stop smoking, hypnosis will make them more receptive to being told to stop. Then, more often then not, they quit the habit.

Now remember that a young child is also in that brainwave. Let us suppose that an adult, such as a parent or teacher, tells them they are useless or stupid, and will always be worthless just like their father. Perhaps the child is told that they are ugly, fat, short, or dim: those words then become core beliefs.

Children who hear parents say things such as, "all the men in our family die young", or "all the women in our family eventually get breast cancer", may embed these beliefs in their subconscious mind, only for them to become major contributors to illness in later life.

I was always told I was unlucky because I had picked up my father's inability to be good at maths, and my mother's inability to grasp English grammar and spelling. My brother was lucky because he understood the subjects in which they were both proficient . Now my parents were actually quite good at both maths and English. Since they each believed they were bad at one or other, and because at an early age I showed little aptitude for either, I gained a very early belief that I was pretty useless in both these departments.

I have since proved to myself that I can actually get by quite well in maths and English as long as I am not asked to spell anything, but it has been a long hard journey for me to change my beliefs. I found out years later that I am actually dyslexic, which is why I often write words and numbers backwards. In the 1950s, however, I was considered stupid by both my parents and my teachers. My parents were actually very loving and I had an excellent upbringing and childhood, but of course they had their own beliefs about what made a child intelligent so these beliefs got passed on to me.

Positive upbringings

We need to learn to really nurture our children. We need to understand how to take care of their minds as well as their bodies. It is important we tell them that they are wonderful, intelligent human beings who will be able to carry out whatever they wish to achieve. They need to always be told that they are special, clever and unique.

I believe a perfect example of a really positive upbringing is Virgin boss, Richard Branson. His mother always told him when he was growing up that he could, and would, be able to accomplish anything and that is exactly what he has done. He trusts in himself and his own judgement, and has shown all of us that everything is possible when you truly believe it is so.

The more we begin to understand that we are one hundred per cent responsible for our own lives, the more we will learn how to take responsibility for everything that happens to us. We need to clear out negative blockages and beliefs, and stop taking on new beliefs that stop us from achieving our true desires.

Negative impact of fear

Fear always stops us doing things: fear of failure, fear of being laughed at, etc. We continually replay our fears and the more we do this the more fearful we become. So we find ourselves on a sort of merry-go-round of fear. This situation also appears to be getting worse as the media continually fuels our fears, especially in financial areas. If we have money we are told that it might lose its value, and if we have no money we are told that we could lose our houses and all our possessions.

Some time ago I made a conscious decision to stop reading newspapers and watching the news on TV because I realised that, apart from actual catastrophes, it was all other people's suppositions of what terrible things may or may not happen next. I remember reading somewhere that the word FEAR is an acronym for False Evidence Appearing Real! Now this did make sense to me.

This fear then creates a new huge negative morphogenic field, which takes on a life of its own and becomes reality in the collective unconscious. This then causes these predictions to actually happen.

Fear is the most destructive force in our society, yet ways are constantly being found to make us more fearful. Just travel through airport security anywhere in the world and you can almost smell the fear that is being instilled in all who travel. Terrorists will always find a way to harm people if that is their intention, and making sure bottles of shampoo or face cream are no larger than a certain size is not going to prevent this. This is about instilling fear and is ridiculous; we need to learn to love everything in our existence and to let the fear go once and for all.

Young people are brought up to fear everything, and of course the more they watch incidents of stabbing and death on TV, whether it is in a movie or on the news, the more their belief systems start to see this as true everyday reality. Then we are surprised by how aggressive young people have suddenly become, and why they are carrying knives and stabbing and shooting one another.

We have to realise that, as a society, we are destroying everything that is beautiful, precious and truthful. We are eliminating joy by always being afraid of the next bad thing that is likely to happen to us. All of this needs to stop if we are to begin to be who we truly are. We must start telling our children from a very young age that the world is a beautiful safe place to live in, where they will be able to create whatever they want in order to always be happy and fulfilled.

Chapter 9: Working With the Inner Child and Belief Systems

I covered how to actually do Inner Child Work in the soul retrieval chapter, as these two things really go hand in hand. However, it is also important to understand how Inner Child Work can help us to deal with so many of our deepest fears. When we learn how to nurture our inner child, and to make that child part of us feel safe and cherished, we begin to look at the world in a very different way. We learn how to create a happy and positive reality for ourselves.

Think about all the times when you were a child and you felt unloved and not listened to. Remember how frustrated you were when your opinion was considered of no significance by people around you. Perhaps you were dismissed and told to go and play, because it was believed by the adults that you had nothing of value to say. How did that feel, belittling, exasperating, and sad perhaps?

This frustrated child is still very much part of you and is still screaming to be heard! Over the years I have come to realise how important it is to work with, and to listen to, our inner child so I have integrated it into the healing work I do. I also touched on this earlier when I talked about abuse.

When we think how many past or parallel lifetimes of abuse, hatred, guilt, frustration and longing for love we have experienced, it is important to understand how many child-like parts of us we need to listen to and learn to reintegrate within our personalities.

John Bradshaw wrote a very good book called *Home Coming*. This does not involve past life work in any way, but it does clearly demonstrate how the frustrated child within us keeps coming to the surface as we persistently play out our frustrations, anxieties and fears. We continually replay situations again and again. Unless we realise why we are doing this and look into what our tantrums are really about, we will just keep re-running them. We get repeatedly angry about the same situations, without realising that this is probably just another repeat of something that upset us when we were a child. Our inner child is screaming to be heard so, unless we start to listen, we will just keep holding on to inner anger and frustrations.

Talking to the inner child

When I work with soul retrieval and especially with cases of abuse, talking to the inner child is imperative. This involves making the child feel safe and loved so that part of them can be unlocked from its time warp of abuse and become a healthy and happy component of that person.

Forgiveness plays such an important part in all of this. We are so hard on ourselves, and so judgemental about other people, that we often forget we are all human. We all make mistakes and we all make errors of judgement. This is what living the earthly experience means.

As I keep reiterating, forgiveness is always a three-way process. It is so important that we learn to forgive other people for how we perceive they have wronged us. We must also ask these people to forgive us for all the anger we have directed towards them, and for anything we have done to hurt them. Then we must also completely forgive ourselves and let go of all our anger about any situation. This is really the only way for us to feel free and live happy, healthy lives.

Trust is also extremely important – trust in ourselves and our ability to make the right decision about people and situations. We are always in the right place at the right time to learn whatever it is we need to learn at that particular moment. If we learn that lesson and then let go of it everything will be fine. However if we are not prepared to understand, the same or a similar situation will be presented to us time and time again. When we are ready to let go of all the guilt, anger, sorrow and pain associated with whatever is hurting us we are finally free to move on.

It is good to ask yourself questions such as: "Why am I experiencing this situation at this particular time?" or "What is being shown to me that I need to work on?" People mirror us all the time for good or bad reasons. They present to us what is deep in our subconscious minds, and what needs to be cleared and dealt with. This can of course be a very positive experience if you look at everyone with love and understanding, but if on a subconscious level you feel unworthy and believe you deserve to be put down, this is exactly what you will attract to you and manifest in your life. I always think that TV programmes, such as *Neighbours from Hell*, are classic examples of this. Each neighbour from hell mirrors the other and attracts 'themselves' into their neighbourhood. Of course the more anger they are sending out to their neighbours the more they are actually attracting to themselves.

Changing negative beliefs

This is why it is so important to change our negative beliefs to positive ones. By holding on to negative beliefs, the only people we are actually hurting is ourselves.

When Vianna Stibal developed Theta Healing she realised that as she worked with different subjects and cured many of their illnesses, she also had to change their beliefs. Unless she found the set of core beliefs that had caused the illness in the first place and changed them, the person's illness would probably reoccur.

How often do doctors operate to replace something like a hip joint? Then a few years later the patient is back to have the other hip done. This is because the patient in question has not dealt with, and released, the emotional problems that caused the need for the hip joint to be replaced in the first place. Whatever instigated this was something deeply embedded in the patient's subconscious mind. As we are talking about a hip joint it is possibly connected to feelings of lack of support and a sense of having nothing to look forward to.

How is it possible, in this age of so called deeper understanding, that we still teach our doctors to look at the mind and body as separate from one another? It is not rocket science that by putting a client into hypnosis and asking them to go back in time to find what is causing the illness, an amazing understanding can often be reached.

Of course there is frequently more than just one cause. For example the person may have a body full of heavy metals and toxins caused by smoking, mercury in their teeth, environmental factors, etc. All of these lower the body's immune system. But by asking the client to look for an understanding of the cause and then finding it, it certainly shows how the mind and body are connected. Frequently with this sort of understanding or real revelation, the client can completely let go of the illness or pain, or at least change in some positive way.

Unless we deal with our emotional problems by working through them and clearing out the cause, we become ill. This is our subconscious mind's way of teaching us to look within and to listen and to learn. It is our deeper self taking drastic measures to get us to wake up and pay attention before it is too late.

Of course this point of view is in definite conflict with what we are taught as children. We are told to hand over our responsibility for healing to something completely outside of ourselves, namely doctors and their bag of pharmaceuticals. This can work well in one way because it creates a morphogenic belief system (if most people believe their doctors and the medicines they prescribe can cure them, they will), so once they start to take the medicine they begin to feel better almost at once. In my opinion this morphogenic belief system is why something like aspirin works. You can find more information about morphogenic belief systems in Rupert Sheldrake's book, *Morphic Resonance.*

Doctors are usually very dedicated people who work extremely hard. They do a tremendous job in non-preventative situations such as when a patient has had an accident, or is already ill. My belief is that the medical profession could do more to prevent sickness developing and then work with their patients to stop a recurrence of the seemingly cured illness.

What can be very worrying is when a doctor tells someone they only have a short time to live- say for example six months. It is usually at this point that the patient gives up completely. Their years of conditioning and belief in doctors will immediately kick in, and they will stop fighting and die exactly around the predicted six month period. I am not blaming the doctors for working in this way because this is how they have been trained.

Taking personal responsibility

What needs to happen is for the patient to take immediate personal responsibility for their illness. I remember Vianna telling me that the reason so many instant healings took place when she worked in Hawaii with the native people was because they all completely believed in her ability to heal them. This then allowed them, with her help, to heal themselves fully.

Too often people go to their family doctor because they are feeling upset and depressed, and they are just prescribed anti-depressants. This is like putting a giant bandage on a wound that hasn't been cleaned out and disinfected. The wound will just keep festering underneath the dressing.

Thank goodness many people are beginning to realise how important it is for them to take charge of their own lives and their own beliefs, rather than just accepting other people's views of the world. Once we all learn to do this we will also be able to find ways to heal our body and our minds quickly and efficiently by ourselves.

We also hold many genetic beliefs that may have been in our families for centuries. You may have been brought up hearing beliefs such as: "All the men in our family die young," or "Everyone in our family eventually dies of a stroke." These views become so engrained in our belief systems that we eventually make them happen, so that then every male member of that specific family will die young, or all people from another family will die of a stroke.

Not all genetic beliefs are negative. I can quote one from my family: we believe our hair will never go grey-so it doesn't. My great-aunt Florrie died aged eighty three, still with dark brown hair: my grandmother died at sixty seven, again still with dark brown hair. My mother's sister Peggy, who is now eighty three, has dark brown hair and my mother at eighty six, still has natural red hair. They all developed a few distinguished grey wisps at the side of their faces when they were in their seventies, but the main bulk of their hair remains the original colour. The hairdresser is often asked how she gets my mother's hair colour to look so good, especially with the grey bits at the side. Women are aghast when they find out she has never dyed her hair.

My own hair still grows its original colour, a sort of nondescript brown, while all of my friends seem to have been battling grey hair since they were in their forties. I go to the hairdresser to have my hair dyed while my friends go to cover up the grey. So there we are - not all family belief systems are bad, and this is one belief I am more than happy to keep! However, the majority of these genetic beliefs can, in the long run, be extremely detrimental to our health.

Our belief systems make us who we are. So it is extremely important that we create a positive reality for ourselves and that we help those around us- especially young children - to do the same. We are who we believe we are. Therefore it is important to stop blaming others for any negative reality we have created.

Chapter 10: Regression Hypnosis to Treat Depression

People often come to see me because they feel depressed and disappointed. The life they had envisioned for themselves is just not happening. They have tried counselling or antidepressants, and some will have been under the care of a psychologist or, in more severe cases, a psychiatrist. Some will feel that the treatment they have received may have helped for a while but many are left floundering and in great distress. This is not, in any way, a reflection on any other healthcare professionals. It is just the way things are. The energy on the planet is changing very rapidly at the moment, so whilst this energy is wonderful for individuals who are spiritually aware, it can be really difficult to handle for those who have no awareness of what is actually happening.

These new energies are all about clearing up old beliefs and outdated ways of being. We are being encouraged by our higher selves to let go of what we don't need and to create what it is we do need. We are leaving third dimensional ways of greed and self-preservation to become part of a higher awareness and more global consciousness.

Regression hypnosis is a wonderful way to help us to do this. We can find out what negative childhood beliefs we are still holding on to, so that by releasing them we can move into our own power. Remember how children up to the age of seven are like sponges and they take everything they are told to be absolute fact. Everything that causes distress and pain in our early years will continually come to the surface in different scenarios, unless we make the inner child part of us feel loved and nurtured.

Therefore, by using regression hypnosis to take the person back into their childhood memories, all the negative feelings and resentments can be completely unlocked, sorted out and forgiven. This work will also give the individual a complete understanding of why they are feeling the way they are, and what is causing their sense of anxiety and depression.

To give an example: a woman may keep feeling really fed up because her husband never seems to have time for her: he is always working. This makes her feel very angry, rejected, upset and unloved. Logically she knows he has to work, but she can't help the way she feels.

If, under hypnosis, I was to ask that same woman to go back into her childhood to find the time when she felt the same emotions, she will probably go into a scene where her mother, her father or both parents are too busy working to spend time with her.

Therefore she is not actually angry with her husband. She has in reality been holding on to these negative emotions since she was a child. Her resentments will keep coming up to the surface unless her inner child is made to feel safe, and until she is able to forgive either one or both of her parents for, as she sees it, their abandonment and neglect of her needs. Logic has absolutely nothing to do with this situation; it is all about the emotions locked in her subconscious mind.

One of the easiest ways to deal with this situation is to tell the client that she is going to allow her adult self to take care of the child that feels so neglected. By showing her how to teach her inner child to feel safe and loved, and by explaining that her father and mother working all the time doesn't mean they didn't love her, she is able to understand that her parents were actually working to look after her.

She is then able to forgive her parents, and then we can invite her lost soul fragment to become reintegrated with the grown up person she is now. She begins to feel loved and whole once again. Once this work is completed the client will no longer feel angry at her husband because she will understand that her original angry feelings were not anything to do with him. She had just attracted his behaviour to her to show that she needed to deal with her childhood issues.

Clearing negative emotions

This is just one example of how, by working in this way, innumerable negative emotions can be brought to the surface and cleared. I suppose you could say that this work is a bit like putting Humpty Dumpty back together again. We are mending all the cracks in the egg and replacing the middle so that no more precious insides or soul fragments can leak out.

This work also permits the individual to clear up negative issues in their own time and at whatever pace is right for them. One way of doing this is to say to the client that the subconscious mind knows and understands exactly what is going on, and why they are feeling depressed. We are going into a corridor and in that corridor are all the doors containing the problems. We are going to systematically work through the different scenes behind the individual doors to sort them out. I also say that once the problem is sorted out the door will completely disappear. They need to be aware that if the doorway doesn't disappear completely they will need to go back into it, as there is more work to do to resolve the issue. This is of course all a metaphor, but it works extremely well.

Some clients will say that there are as many as fifteen to twenty doors causing the problem, whilst others will say three or four. I tell them that this is all rather like peeling an onion, and just the correct number of doorways will appear for us to deal with in each individual session. This allows the client's subconscious mind to prioritise and focus on the most urgent issues in each session. Also, by working in this way, quicker results are achieved because the most urgent issues are dealt with first.

This work can be heavy both for the client and for the therapist, especially if a lot of childhood violence or abuse is involved. However it does bring fantastic results, enabling the client to feel in complete control of their life; probably for the first time ever! It also helps the person to understand why they have been feeling so bad for so long and the real reason for their anger, depression or anxiety. It teaches them to recognise the power of forgiveness, and to ultimately heal themselves by taking personal responsibility for their own actions. They have to realise that only they themselves can clean up their own act and create a happy and positive life. This can only happen with the complete release of childhood trauma and by practising forgiveness of self and others.

Schooldays are traumatic for many children, especially if they are bullied either by their teachers or by other pupils. This same method of letting the adult sort out what is happening to the child, allows years of pent up anger, loneliness and pain to be released, while at the same time permitting the inner child to reintegrate with the adult self.

Inner child work is of absolute, fundamental importance. If you take an antidepressant it may alleviate the problem for a short while, but the rot is still going on underneath. Once you have learnt how to nurture your inner child, and how to forgive everything from your past, then lost soul fragments can be brought back and you will never need to suffer from depression again.

Mirroring our deepest insecurities

This understanding can be taken further when we recognise how people mirror our deepest insecurities back to us. If we believe on a deep core level, that we are unworthy and unlovable, we will inevitably attract a partner who makes us feel that way. Remember how angry the lady was with her husband? Actually he was just serving as a mirror, allowing her to understand what it was she needed to look into and release from her past.

Chapter 11:   Finding Ourselves and
Finding Joy

Freedom is something we gain when we begin to understand ourselves and the key to freedom is learning to love one another as we should love ourselves.

We are taught to believe that happiness is outside of ourselves. This is not true, and unless we can gain the freedom of understanding that it is us who attract and create everything in our lives, we can never be free. To other people we project love, hatred, sadness, guilt, anger, rage, indifference, to name but a few. Some of these emotions we may be aware of and others we are sending out on a deep subconscious level. So often we say things such as: "It is all his fault," or "Everyone is against me," without realising that everything that is happening to us is actually a mirror of our subconscious. We are attracting people and situations into our lives so that we can actually work through, and work out, what is really going on with us on a far deeper level.

One of the reasons I work with hypnosis, more than any other healing tool, is that it gives me a way of letting my clients really understand what is actually going on with them on a far deeper level. If you ask someone a question whilst they are in hypnosis you are far more likely to get the correct answer; especially if rhetorical language is used. Whilst in hypnosis it is much easier for the client to see and understand why, for example, they have a deep mistrust of someone.

This person may not have done anything that they are consciously aware of to hurt them, but they know not to trust them. In hypnosis the client can easily discover the reason for these negative emotions. Once this understanding has been reached, then a solution can immediately be found to resolve and dissolve, whatever the issue was between these two people.

What people do not usually understand is that by changing themselves, they change what they are projecting to the outside world, so the relationship between themselves and others begins to change. The more we can find oneness in ourselves the more balanced we will feel, and the more fulfilling our lives will become.

We have experienced thousands of past lives. If you start to think how many times you have been angry and upset with yourself, and others in this lifetime, just think how much anger, guilt and resentment you may also be holding from past lives.

Making peace with ourselves and others

Once we resolve these things, as and when they come up, we no longer need to repeat them. Once we realise that the only true way to oneness is by total forgiveness of self and of others we can let so much go. It is vital to forgive others for all the things they may have done to hurt us, and it is equally important to ask them to forgive us for all the suffering we have caused them. We must also forgive ourselves for everything that is in any way connected to whatever the circumstances are. This is why we keep meeting up with the same souls again and again. Until we make total peace with them, and resolve whatever needs to be resolved, the same type of situation will keep presenting itself lifetime after lifetime.

Forgiveness is such a fundamental part of healing; there is really no sense in just taking someone back into a past life if the therapist doesn't help the person resolve the problems that are connected to that lifetime. The client's subconscious mind always takes them into a particular lifetime for a good reason, so it is very important for the therapist to help the client to get to the heart of the issue so that the client can be free of it.

Compassion is always the key and it is always a three-way process: unreservedly forgiving the person or the event that caused the problem, asking them for total forgiveness and then absolute forgiveness for yourself. I know I keep on and on about forgiveness, but until all of this has been done the situation cannot be laid to rest. Often there are many lifetimes where the same scenario is played out again and again. Unless all of these lifetimes are resolved, and everything that is in any way connected to them is sorted out, the situation will continue to replay in this lifetime in some form or another. There are always many aspects to just one problem so it is imperative to remove all the negative layers.

Things are moving so quickly at the moment that we often find ourselves trying to sort out what seems like millions of problems at the same time. It is always good to remember that your higher self will never present you with more than you can cope with at any particular time. Although saying that, you may well be stretched just about as far as you can go for your own greater good.

We have chosen our life's lessons and, even if these sometimes seem insurmountable when we are in the middle of them, once we come out of all the pain and heartache we are usually much stronger individuals. If you look back at the times in your life when everything seemed impossible, and then you remember what you did and how you coped to sort out a situation, you will realise how much stronger and more resolute you are now that it is over.

Standing in our own power

Of course if we don't learn from these difficult situations we will just get presented with them, over and over again, until we get whatever it was all about. This is how our soul teaches us to become stronger and to stand in our own power.

If we continually give up our power, for example to the military or to another person, such as a spouse, we need to look inside ourselves to find out why we are doing it. We need to ask ourselves questions such as: "why do I constantly feel the need to be told what to do", or "why do I just do whatever this person tells me", or "why does this person feel the need to put me down and why do I accept it?" We can also be afraid of particular objects, such as a lift or a plane, or perhaps an institution such as a hospital. All of these questions will bring up unresolved issues related to that person or object.

Sometimes when I feel unnerved by someone or something, I will just sit in meditation and ask to be shown what the root cause is. I will often see myself in a particular situation as a child. Or on occasions I will go into a past life and find out what is still causing me to feel upset. I then do all the relevant forgiveness and cut all the etheric cords that may still be causing me a problem.

All over the world people are finding relationships more difficult to deal with in this time. Let us call it time, but the more you become at one with this work the more you become aware that time as we know it really does not exist at all. Everything is going on at the same time, which is why we are so affected by our so-called past lives. Unless we resolve whatever is going on with us in other dimensions and times these issues will continue to affect us.

We have experienced many lives as men and women. I always find it funny how women never have any issue with this, but how often men look at me in absolute horror when I tell them not to be too surprised if they should happen to see themselves in either a male or a female body during the regression. I tell them to just go with it and see what unfolds. All of these lifetimes teach us different things. We also experience lives when we are rich and powerful and lives when we are poor and seemingly defenceless. All of this helps to teach us all the different aspects of ourselves, and how to always be 'at one' no matter what our outer surroundings may appear to be.

Opportunities are so much greater now. Once upon a time we would meet and usually stay with one specific person, happily or not, for a complete lifetime. Travel for most ordinary people was on foot or horseback, so to journey more than a few miles at a given time was almost unheard of. We lived our lives in a specific area, usually with one particular person and perhaps their relatives, until we died or were killed.

New freedoms, new relationships

Now, with the advent of aeroplanes, telephones, television, the internet and freedom for men and women in the western world, we are able to connect with many different people from far off places on literally a daily basis. This is of course wonderful but, at the same time, because we have so much freedom we are rarely content to stay in one place with just one person any more. This often leads to the traditional family unit being broken up and children with mothers and fathers living sometimes far away from one another. We are no longer content with what we see as 'our lot'.

All of this of course opens up wonderful opportunities for our souls to learn. At the same time we can very easily find our whole lives turned upside down when we deem ourselves happily married to someone, yet we find someone else coming into our lives who we also feel great love for.

Often clients come to see me because they find themselves in love with two people at the same time. This is not really surprising when you consider how many lifetimes we have experienced, and how many people we have loved over eons of time. The client has usually made oaths and vows to both of these people. Perhaps to love, cherish, obey, to always be there for that person, to always find that person, etc. No wonder they don't know who or how to choose between them!

It is always a good idea to remember that everyone who comes into our life does so for a reason. Only when we are finally clear of all negative memories will we be able to know that we are all one, all interconnected by divine love and inspiration.

I always find it fascinating, when I work with clients and their most difficult relationships, to see how the person begins to understand why they are with a specific person. Once they are able to finalise and release the issues in the relationship, they are free to either stay with that individual or move on.

Yes of course we can be with a person we have loved over eons of time, and who is probably a member of our soul group. Nevertheless the people who are part of our soul groups are also the ones we trust to teach us our most difficult lessons; we frequently choose them as partners when we have a particularly difficult lesson to learn. We often let them hurt us the most in order to teach us the most.

Sometimes two souls choose to grow together. They may marry in order to fulfil a promise and to bring a specific child into the world, or they may work together to create something with the aim that it will help all. These people often experience tough lessons, but they experience everything together as a unit of two.

When I think of a perfect love match I often think of the Italian film director Federico Fellini and his wife Giulietta Masina. He is best known for films such as *La Strada, La Dolce Vita* and *Roma;* she was known as his anima (soul) by Italian film goers. They met when he was 23, and she later took the female lead in many of his films. She was the perfect expression of his artistic creativity: they were together everyday, and when he died she passed very quickly after him. They had obviously chosen to work together to bring his cinematic art form to the world. He was a man far ahead of his time and his view of the world is now reflected in our understanding of quantum physics. An example of this is something he is quoted as saying when referring to his films: "Everyone lives in his own fantasy world, but most people don't understand that. No one perceives the *real* world. Each person simply calls his private, personal fantasies the Truth. The difference is that I *know* I live in a fantasy world. I prefer it that way and resent anything that disturbs my vision." (Fellini in *I, Fellini*, ed. by Charlotte Chandler, 1995)

Another example is Winston Churchill and his wife Clementine. He was not the easiest of men, but she was always there to sustain him as he brought England victoriously out of World War Two. She helped and supported him while he found the strength to do what he needed to do.

People can work together either as a perfect expression of their art, or for their country, or just to fulfil something they both want to accomplish. All of this is so that the soul can continue to grow.

Outgrowing relationships

When people start to work on their issues they often outgrow existing relationships, especially if the other person in the partnership is not prepared to look inside themselves. A man may be deeply in love with a woman at 20 but find that he has nothing in common with her by the time he is 35. This could be because the couple have promised each other to bring a certain soul into the world, and the job is then done. This may well have cleared up whatever past life issues they had and they are now both free to move on. Or maybe just one of the couple has developed more spiritually or intellectually, and the other person is just as they were. Alternatively they could have both developed in completely different directions and may not be compatible any more.

There is no shame in this as it is just about starting a new phase and moving into it. We have to learn to stop holding on to people just because we are afraid what may happen to us once we let them go. We have to grow in whatever way is right for us. We need to learn to trust that our higher selves will always take us in the direction we need to go in for our individual good. Times may sometimes be hard but it is important to look at difficulties as opportunities to learn. The more we welcome new things and put out positive creative energy the better our lives will automatically become.

Often when a new partner comes into our life it is because the old relationship is finished and whatever needed to be done together is finished. Or it is because at least one person in the relationship is ready for a new challenge. Perhaps the partner who is left needs to be on their own for a bit to examine what went wrong, and to come to terms with what it is they really need from a relationship.

Often we need to be on our own for a while, especially if we are on a fast track spiritual path. The more exploratory work you do on yourself the more you will change. In five years time you may be in a very different place than you are now. Is it really fair to expect someone to live with you whilst you go through such dramatic changes, unless of course the other person is also doing the same work and is changing just as rapidly as you are?

I know from personal experience that many things I believed in twenty years ago I now view very differently. Lots of my core beliefs have changed dramatically, especially in the past eight years, since I have been doing this work. Each time I changed I believed that I had all the answers. Now I understand that this is all about perspective. The way I view myself, and the world I live in, changes radically every time I clear out more of my old negative and outdated beliefs. Everything is moving and changing all the time and we just need to accept that and go with it. When we feel blocked in our lives it is because we do not listen to that inner voice inside our heads. We need to trust more, so that the energies we attract will bring in positive experiences.

Learning from my clients

My work is also always changing, which is why I may teach lots of workshops in one year, and then the next year I may not want to teach any at all. I may choose to go to a lot of workshops run by other people, or I may decide to just work on a one-to-one basis with clients. This way of working allows me to learn from new and fascinating teachers, and to incorporate new and exciting techniques into my work.

My clients are also like teachers to me since, as I work intuitively, I find that I develop new and exciting ways to help them to clear out their problems. This is never something I plan to do. I am guided to work in a certain way and it just happens. These new methods then become something I naturally incorporate into my work.

I recognise that the way I work has changed dramatically and definitely for the better, over the past eight years. By learning different methods of healing from other healers and teachers, I can take from these what I feel is right for me to use with my own clients. The more tools I have the more chance I have of reaching a wider audience, and of helping more people. Quite possibly five years from now I will be using a slightly different way of working. This will of course depend on how much I learn and how that can help me to help my clients.

We all continue to learn valuable information from one another; for example, Neuro Linguistic Programming (NLP) was developed by Richard Bandler and John Grinder studying methods used by people such as Milton Erickson, Virginia Satir and Fritz Perls. Perls, who developed Gestalt therapy, was himself heavily influenced by Wilhelm Reich, Jan Smuts, and Alfred Korzybski among others.

One of the things I was told when I was training was that my clients would always reflect my own issues. This wasn't something that I think I particularly believed at the time, but it is certainly something that has proved to be the case over and over again. This also means that the more I can clear my own issues the more I can help my clients to clear theirs.

Hooponopono

Dr Hew Ihaleakala Len is the principal practitioner and teacher in the world today of the Hawaiian Hooponopono system; an ancient Hawaiian practice of reconciliation and forgiveness, He learned the process from Morrnah Simeona, a Hawaiian healer who was given the title "National Treasure".

Dr Hew Len first attracted media attention when, using Hooponopono, he cured all the patients in a mental hospital. He believes that if something is brought to his attention it is because, in some way, it reflects something he needs to heal within himself. When he first went to work as a psychiatrist in the mental hospital in Honolulu, Hawaii, he found the patients were violent both with other patients and with the employees. The general staff stayed away whenever they could and the paint wouldn't stop peeling off the walls. Within a short time of Dr Hew Len being in the hospital and working on himself daily, everything began to change. The staff no longer stayed away, patients started to get better and the paint stopped coming off the walls. After three years the hospital closed down because no-one was ill any more. Such is the power of Hooponopono!

I have also practiced Hooponopono on myself and seen a change in my clients, so I can also attest to it working. In Los Angeles I remember a colleague of mine, who attended the Hooponopono course with me, telling me how he had practised Hooponopono for an hour on the train as he was coming to work. He was due to work with a client whom he had worked with before and knew to be difficult. He phoned me later to tell me that it was one of the best sessions he had ever had, and all the issues the client had been experiencing were cleared.

The clearer we are the more we are able to channel in light. If we are coming from a place of darkness or anger how are we to teach others to bring light and happiness into their own lives?

As therapists we have a personal responsibility to always try to do the best for our clients at all times. That also means looking to heal ourselves from within. It worries me how many people train and practise such things as hands on healing, hypnotherapy, EFT, past life regression, psychotherapy, etc. without at least attempting to clear out some of their own emotional problems first.

I truly believe that the right client always finds the therapist they were meant to find. It is important for the healer to not only work with the client to the best of their ability, but to also ask themselves why this particular client has chosen to come to them with this specific problem. What is there in the therapist that also needs to be understood and cleared?

By this I do not mean that if I am treating an alcoholic client I am likely to have a drink problem. However it could well mean that during the time I work with that person, something in the way they see the world, or the way they behave in relation to a certain situation may well, on some level, relate to something that I have experienced in my own life.

I may not understand or have any idea what it is, but as I have mentally asked my guides to help me clear out anything that comes up, I believe that what needs to clear will be released automatically; or a situation will be brought to my attention in some way to help me to understand what I need to release.

Dreams are a very good way of doing this. If I have a very vivid dream I know something is coming up. I often get clients who come to me and tell me that either they have been getting the same recurring dream since they were a child, or that recently they keep getting the same dream over and over again.

Once the person is in hypnosis it becomes very clear that whatever this dream is, it is something to be cleared and sorted. It may be something that happened in childhood but more often than not it relates to a past life experience. Once the forgiveness has been done, the oaths and vows let go of, and the soul fragment is where it needs to be, the dream stops. It is really just our subconscious mind telling us to sort something out, and once we do it we can move on.

Books and films sometimes bring up issues, as do news items. If you are deeply affected by something you read or see, it is reflecting something on a deeper level that rests within you. By this I don't mean major events such as Tsunamis or earthquakes, where many people lose their lives, as these affect us all deeply. I mean something very specific that acts as a trigger for our past memories.

Many years ago I remember reading a book about the old Hawaii long before it became an American State. When it was time for a leader of a specific community to die he or she would just go out to sea in a boat, and then just leave their body. Why this affected me so deeply I had no idea, but it was something about which I felt a deep understanding.

I have always been drawn to Hawaii and remember watching Jack Lord in *Hawaii Five-0* on the television when I was a teenager. When I actually went to Hawaii a few years ago I was disappointed. Not because it wasn't beautiful- it was; it was just not how I either imagined it or perhaps remembered it from a past life.

It just didn't feel right somehow. The flowers were enormous, the birds and the wild life were stunning, but it was all very American. Now, I absolutely love America and I go there whenever I can, either for courses or just to visit, but somehow my soul cried out for the real Hawaii as I had always imagined it – very spiritual with an ethereal quality.

Many people believe that the ancient island of Lemuria was where the Hawaiian Islands are today. When it sank, just islands were left. Who knows? This may be true.

After flying into Honolulu Airport, which is on the Island of Oahu, I took a small plane to the Island of Kauai. This is where the original film of *South Pacific* was filmed. Many other films were also made there, including the beach scene in *The Thorn Birds* with Richard Chamberlain, and *Six Days, Seven Nights* with Harrison Ford, who allegedly lands a plane on a desert island. A lot of scenes from *Jurassic Park* were filmed on the island as well. It is a stunning place.

I went up in a helicopter and flew all over the Island, and then took a four-hour boat trip in one of those rafts of the type the Navy Seals use. It was unforgettable and exhilarating. I saw dolphins, whales and the rare green turtle. I was so lucky, so why did I feel so dissatisfied and unnerved? It made absolutely no sense at all: that is until two very different experiences happened to me.

The first one occurred when I was in Miami for a Matrix Energetics course run by Dr Richard Bartlett. I had already met up with a group of friends that I had previously met when I attended Richard's course in Baltimore. We decided to take the learning experience even further and join up this time for the complete three-part course. One of the group, whose name is Mark, I found particularly fascinating because not only had he lived on Hawaii, he is also a mine of information on just about everything else.

Since Baltimore I had already done a bit of work with him on the phone and when we met up again one of the first things he said to me was: "Liz, do you know you work just like a Hawaiian?" I was very surprised because at that time I had no conscious idea how Hawaiians worked.

Then something interesting happened in my hotel in Miami. I noticed this young Hawaiian man who was also attending the course. He kept playing two pipes, which evidently form an ancient Hawaiian musical instrument, whilst standing behind someone. The man was sitting down and had a pipe placed on each of his shoulders. Both looked as if they were in a trancelike state. I watched him do this with a few people, and they all said how relaxed they felt after the experience.

I didn't really think any more about this until later in the day when the musician came up to me. He called me "auntie", which seemed odd, especially as I had already seen him ask the names of other people and then call them by their name. He told me that his guides had instructed him to find me so he could play the pipes for me. I felt honoured and I readily agreed.

I sat down and he stood behind me placing the pipes on my shoulders. The moment he started to play I was transformed. The tears started rolling down my cheeks and I went into a deep meditative state. I saw myself surrounded by native Hawaiian people who were all fondly wishing me farewell as I set off on my own in a small boat. The reason this scene in the book had brought up so much emotion for me was because I was tapping into one of my own memories.

The second incident happened whilst I was on a Hooponopono course in Los Angeles. I was talking to Keith, the husband of the course organiser. He is Hawaiian and a really lovely man; before long I found myself telling him about my disappointment with Oahu and Kauai. He looked at me, smiled and said: "You were on the wrong Island. Your Island is Maui. That is the Island where you lived when you were a Kahuna healer and leader." He is very psychic so I told him about the book and the man with the pipes. He smiled and told me it was exactly what happened when it was my time to leave my body in that lifetime. At last the picture was coming together and things started to make sense.

One final piece to that puzzle was added when I sat in meditation and asked to be given my Hawaiian name. I was told it was Mahana:

this was not a name that made any sense to me so I put the word into Google. Lo and behold, it is a Hawaiian name meaning Sunshine and there is a place on the Island of Maui called Mahana. The power of all of this stuff never fails to amaze me. It helps me to understand how little we really know, and how little we understand about ourselves and our universe. I haven't yet been to Maui but I know that when I do, all that I have been told will prove to be true.

Being joyful

We seem to have forgotten what joy is. I believe when we lived a more primitive existence we seemed to be more connected with nature, and who we really were. This allowed us to trust our deeper instincts more. Now, because we are brought up listening to so many other opinions, we have lost our connection with who we truly are; we just believe all that is fed to us on television and in the media.

We also seem to have forgotten what it feels like to know we are truly safe. As I explained before, a child up to the age of seven is always in either the alpha or the theta brainwave. Therefore when everything they hear is about people attacking one another, and how terrible all the financial situations are everywhere, how else can they interpret the world but in a pessimistic way? Joy can be just sitting under a tree and experiencing a beautiful sunset, or watching your child smile as he plays with his dog in the sunshine. We should feel joy everyday, not just on rare occasions when something good happens. We now seem to look for the negative side of everything.

A woman who really knows how to experience joy is Andrea Jaeger and she does this by dedicating her life to helping children with cancer. When you talk to Andrea she absolutely radiates joy and light. Once a well known tennis player, she had to give it all up when a shoulder injury forced her out of the game. Rather than despairing about what had happened to her successful career she decided to put all the money she had earned into creating the

Little Star Cancer Foundation. She bought a ranch and created week-long breaks where children with cancer can go and meet up with other children with the illness. They can just forget their sickness and have a wonderful time. Often the families of these children have so little because so much of what they owned has gone into paying for treatments. The families get a short break and the children meet up with people who really understand what they are going through, but at the same time are able to show them how to really enjoy themselves.

Andrea and her helpers are coming from a place of pure joy. The children feel at total peace on the ranch possibly for the first time since the start of their illness. They make lots of new friends with whom they are able to stay in contact through email and telephone calls. They leave the ranch feeling loved, supported and no longer alone in their struggle with cancer.

Andrea is a remarkable woman who has been running the charity for over twenty years with a combination of pure love, light, joy and dogged determination. She and her staff are doing a fantastic job for these children.

We can always find joy in helping others but it can also come from something much simpler. Recently when I travelled to Virginia, I arrived at my old colonial-style guesthouse late at night. My first sight on arrival was of two deer grazing on the lawn in the moonlight. Then when I woke up in the morning I looked out of the window to see the sun on the Blue Ridge Mountains. All of these things brought up a feeling of pure joy in me. It was all so beautiful and I really felt a sensation of absolute peace, and the feeling of being at one with nature. I went out and stood on the porch to be greeted by two dogs and the smell of freshly brewed coffee. This was fantastic, especially when later it was served together with home made waffles, syrup, fruit and fresh cream. This was just bliss!

Many of us seem to have forgotten what joy is. I was recently talking to a friend about a lovely week I spent in Corfu in the beautiful resort of Kommeno. I was enthusiastic about it because the hotel, the food, the sea and all the facilities were amazing. Her first words to me were: "Well, what didn't you like about it? There must be something you needed to complain about." I was amazed; I had spent a faultless week in the sun, and here was someone assuming that nothing could ever be perfect. To me this was very sad, and brought home to me how many people look for faults in everything and everyone. If we go somewhere and look for the bad this is always what we will find. If we look at everything as a beautiful experience this is what we will create.

What are we doing to our children when we look for the negative rather than the positive in situations? The glass is always half empty rather than half full. Is that not sad? TV programmes do this all the time: for example, 95% of the news contains negative forecasts about what terrible thing is bound to happen next.

I am convinced that recessions, and other economic problems, are made far worse by TV and newspapers creating a negative morphogenic field of fear. Create enough fear in enough people and this will automatically become part of the creative unconscious. The more people begin to worry about how everything *MAY* come crashing down around them, the more they themselves will bring this into their own lives. We create our own reality, so we must be careful not to buy into all of this rubbish and therefore create pessimistic patterns in our own lives. It is so easy to become fearful, and it is also often very difficult to stay positive and uplifted when all of this is going on around us.

When we refuse to accept all of this nonsense our lives will improve very quickly. My own life has changed dramatically since I stopped believing that everything that is out there is totally beyond my control. If I don't watch the news and read everyone else's negative beliefs in a newspaper, my subconscious mind doesn't inadvertently buy into them.

Of course I am aware that many terrible things continue to happen in the world today. But I also know that we have to stop them rather than reinforce them. Mother Theresa said that she would never attend an anti-war rally. She would only attend a peace rally. By saying this she completely understood how important it is to focus on the positive rather than the negative i.e. peace rather than war.

We must continue to remember that our young children are always in a form of hypnosis, so we must create a positive world for them to grow up in. The Jesuit priests understood this all too well. Remember the Jesuit saying: "Give me a child until the age of seven and I will show you the man"? These men knew they could influence young children by continually indoctrinating them until they began using the beta brainwave, the brainwave of reason, at about seven years old. This is also why so many young men brought up in the priesthood stayed in it for life, as their core belief systems became based on the Jesuit doctrine.

Chapter 12: New Country, Different Beliefs

During the course of my work I have noticed how people's belief systems vary considerably depending on which continent they grow up in. People from different countries have completely different outlooks on life. For example, if you are a little girl who grows up in a country where women are considered to be second class citizens you will probably feel put down, unworthy and not as good as your male counterparts. Logically you may know that this is not the case, but your subconscious mind will still hold the belief that somehow being a man makes you a much more worthy person. I notice this especially when I work with women from some of the Middle Eastern countries. A part of them really wants to feel free and to be standing in their own power; whilst everything in their belief systems and their culture is working against them to resist them making this change.

Culture and marriage

In countries such as India, Bangladesh and Pakistan, children are usually brought up to respect their parent's views on marriage. Men and women are often expected to go into arranged marriages with the person chosen for them by their family. I have noticed how this causes a real dilemma for many of my clients. Their parents send them abroad to study or to work, guaranteeing that they become highly educated individuals. Then they are expected to go home, to conform and marry the person chosen by the family.

These people are holding on to all their childhood beliefs that they have to do what is expected of them,, but at the same time they want to ensure their own happiness by marrying the person of their choice. When they do conform they are unhappy, when they refuse they are unhappy, so they often believe they have no way out. I really sympathise with these people because they want to do what is best for them, but they don't want to upset their families who have often made huge sacrifices to educate them.

Some people live though traumatic childhoods, which can still affect them greatly as adults. If you live in constant fear of being bombed, or not having enough food or water, of course it is going to influence your outlook on life. We only have to look at some of the African and Middle Eastern countries that are continually ravaged by unrest and war, to see how unsettling it must be to be brought up in these countries.

When I work in countries such as Italy or Ireland I see a very strong belief in the healing power of God and the angels, but at the same time a contrasting fear of being punished by the devil, or of ending up in hell if they do something wrong.

Brazil, and some of the African countries, are great believers in voodoo and magic. People are often holding on to strong beliefs of cursing others, and of being cursed, as a result of living within these cultures. From a very early age their subconscious minds take this on board, leading them to create the appropriate events to reinforce their usually very negative beliefs.

In complete contrast Hawaii is the land of instant healings, where people believe in total forgiveness. Therefore, when they go to someone who they trust can help them they are very often instantly healed of their affliction.

I lived for many years in Italy where children are generally happy, because Italians love children and are prepared to nurture their talents from a very young age. Children feel important in Italy so they usually grow into confident adults.

Expressing our beliefs

The UK is different and quite an emotionally cold place to grow up in. When I was a small child in Bristol many people had the old belief that children should be seen and not heard. As a consequence many children grew up feeling unable to speak up for what they believed in.

Most Americans are positive people. They seem to believe that they can accomplish absolutely anything, and this is great for children because they are brought up without fear, feeling that they will be able to achieve whatever they most want in life. Their belief systems create who they are and they get what they want.

In Britain, adults are inclined to always assume the worst about everything, but in my experience Italians and Americans are much more positive, so it must be down to the difference in their early years. I am using British, Italian and American examples because these are the countries I have either lived in or visited the most.

I notice the difference when I travel on trains. In Britain we all ignore one another, even if we travel on the same train together for years. We only say "good morning" if someone says it to us first, which of course they never do. When we pass someone in a hotel corridor or in a lift we just bow our heads and think our private thoughts. I often make a point of saying good morning just so I can see the look of surprise on the face of the other person.

In Italy people talk to each other, and often share food if the journey is long and they are not planning to use the restaurant carriage. It is normal to say "good day" or "good evening" wherever you are.

In America people are also much more open. Some years ago my mother and I spent a week at the house of an American friend of mine. Everyday, in order to go into Central Manhattan, we commuted to and from Ronconcoma on Long Island. It was just after 9/11 and the American nation was deep in shock, but they still went out of their way to be friendly. These people travelled to and from work every day and they all talked to one another. By the second day they started to include my mother and me in their conversations. They had never met us, but just because we were travelling with them every day we were included. We were offered beer and invited to join in card games, so we were quickly made to feel really welcome on "their" train.

In American hotels and lifts people always speak to one another. To be friendly to one another is the norm wherever you are. This must a better way to bring up our children rather than the sense of reserve we British seem to have. Perhaps it is covering up a fear in some way – fear of being ignored or refused. Whatever it is, it is not positive for us or for visitors to the UK.

When people are regressed using hypnosis it can be interesting to notice how sometimes their characters and mannerisms change as their nationality changes.

I have hypnotised people who went back to a previous life as a Nazi and are British or American in this lifetime, or people who were white and are now black, and vice versa. This is why racial prejudice is just so absurd. When we show hatred to our fellow man we are actually showing hatred to ourselves.

Strong connections

One of my most interesting cases involved a lady born of a white mother and black father. Her partner is Indian and quite a bit younger than her. They have been together for a long time and are very happy together.

She sold a house near London that she loved and then moved to Bristol because she had a very strong connection with the city, and really felt that this was were she needed to be. I met (let us call her Pauline) when she was going through a Kundalini rising.

A Kundalini rising is when a coiled serpent-like energy in the lower back rushes through the Chakras up into the crown, then sort of explodes all at once. This can be an intensely wonderful spiritual experience for some who have been working to achieve this. They feel joy, ecstasy and an explosion of light they never thought possible.

However, for those who are not ready and do not understand what is going on, it can be truly terrifying. The person may start to undergo out of body experiences; their whole body might start to shake and they can have intense feelings of terror. Unresolved past lives sometimes start to come up all at once, and the person starts seeing other dimensions. This can actually be a frightening experience for people who know and understand what is happening to them, but for someone who has never even considered the spiritual path it can be the equivalent of hell on earth.

Thank goodness psychiatrists are starting to recognise what this is but, not so long ago, people who exhibited these symptoms were considered insane by their doctors and immediately interned in a mental institution. The person, and their relatives, naturally trusted the opinion of the doctors, so they too believed that they were now completely mad. Hazel Courteney wrote a book on the subject, which she called *Divine Intervention*. She experienced her own Kundalini rising whilst going up an escalator in Harrods department store in London. Her book tells of her quest to understand, and come to terms with, what had happened to her.

Going back to my client; Pauline was also quite upset with Bristol as a city. She felt particularly incensed by the slavery that began there in the 15th Century. It wasn't abolished until after Thomas Clarkson came to the city in 1787 and started a campaign to eradicate it.

I knew that it was probable that this love-hate relationship with Bristol was tied to the slave trade in some way, so I told her to travel back in time and find out what all this pent-up anger was about.

She immediately went back to a life as a young girl in Africa. She and her brother were stolen by slave traders and put on a ship. She found herself in Bristol where she and her brother were separated, and sold to two different merchants. The brother seems to have died fairly quickly whilst, even though she was badly treated and kept in a damp basement, she seems to have lived longer.

Pauline told me how, for some time, she had been hearing the voice of a man who kept telling her what to do. She felt sure it was her brother from that lifetime. We discovered many oaths and vows tying the slave girl and her brother together. It was important to release all of these before sending the brother, who was earthbound and still hanging around, to the light.

The soul fragment belonging to Pauline was also stuck, so we released all the oaths and vows of vengeance she had made to the people who had hurt her. Then she completely forgave them, and asked them to forgive her, for all the anger and negativity she had been sending out to them. Then she forgave herself for everything she needed to let go of from that life. I asked her if that fragment needed to stay in the light or come back to her, and she told me that it needed to come back. We then reintegrated the healed soul fragment back with her.

The client always knows what needs to happen to the soul fragment – whether it needs to stay in the light or be reintegrated back with them: it is just a matter of trusting what the person says and then asking that it be done. Over the years I have learnt that the best way for me to do this is with Theta Healing.

I also had a very strong feeling that this was not all, and that there was a lot more stuff still connected with Bristol to come up. I asked her whether this was the only lifetime connected to the slave trade, or was there perhaps something else she needed to resolve?

She immediately flipped into a life where she became a young white girl living with her rich family in Royal York Crescent, Clifton, in Bristol. What is particularly interesting about this case is that in this life Pauline had chosen to rent a flat a little further along the same crescent.

The girl's father was a very successful merchant who kept two young slaves in the house – a boy and a girl. He was treating both the slaves badly and was sexually abusing the little black girl. The daughter was very upset and unhappy about what was going on in her family. She felt very sorry for both the slaves who were kept underneath the house in the cold and damp stable area, and was very angry at her father for abusing his power. I asked her if she recognised any of these people from this lifetime, and she immediately told me that the father is also her father today who is now black. The little slave girl is her mother today, who in this lifetime is white, and the little black boy is her Indian partner today.

Once she understood all of this, she was able to release all the anger and guilt about what had happened and being unable to do anything about it. She could also understand that all the fury she was feeling about the slave trade in Bristol was her own rage at her father, and what had been going on in his household.

Interestingly, her partner told me later that he had never felt comfortable living in Royal York Crescent. He said he often felt uneasy, almost as if he shouldn't be there, whenever he walked along the high pavement running the length of the elevated area where the houses are. The old stables, where the slave children were kept, are now garages adjacent to the road and are underneath this pavement area.

Pauline has always had a difficult relationship with both her parents in this lifetime: however things have started to improve. It is interesting how we change colour and ethnicity in order to learn, and to understand, more about ourselves and others.

Affinities to people and places

We appear to have experienced a wide spectrum of different cultures but at the same time we are frequently born into the same country time and again. Perhaps this is because we feel a particular affinity towards it, or we may have made oaths and vows of allegiance to it.

As I mentioned before, most of the past lives I have since experienced in regression have been in Italy. I have seen a few in England, Egypt, Hawaii and one that could be somewhere in the Ottoman empire, probably Turkey, where I was a young girl who was stolen from a horse-drawn wooden cart by a man, and whisked off to a harem. Interestingly I know the man in this life as he is now a friend of mine. And remember the English male doctor amputating limbs during the Crimean war? I was probably also some sort of officer with an allegiance to England at that time.

Once, while I was attending a Theta Healing course in Rome, I promised to do a hypnotherapy session with a man called Sergio with whom I felt a particular connection. I felt I knew him very well, although logically I knew that I didn't because I had only just met him.

When I hypnotised him he went straight back to Atlantis, and I had one of the strangest sensations I had ever felt working with someone. I felt such an intimate connection with him that before I had time to think, the words: "I know you, don't I?" came out of my mouth. He was in deep hypnosis and looked at me with a rather puzzled expression and said: "Of course you know me, you are my wife. Why are you asking me if I know you or not? I should know you because I am married to you."

Well, that explained why I felt such a strong connection with him. This man has since become one of my true friends, and although we are not romantically involved in this lifetime, there is still a deep feeling of love and trust between us. I have subsequently hypnotised him on many other occasions, and we are also married in many of the lifetimes we have been shown.

Vianna Stibal also hypnotised me a few years later when I was in America. I went straight back to a lifetime where I was being taken to marry a man who was much older than me. I was not happy about the age difference, but after I met him I stayed with him for the whole of that lifetime because of the deep respect I felt for him. The man in that lifetime is Sergio in this.

Chapter 13: Creativity and Famous Regressions

Children are naturally creative. This may be because they have a natural talent for something, or just because they are tuning into the collective unconscious. When we are very young we do not question, we just accept the knowledge we are receiving. The older we get the more we are inclined to stop listening to our true creative self, and listen instead to what others keep telling us we should do. On occasions we even stop ourselves from doing something we really love without understanding our reasons for doing it.

Angela didn't understand why, since the birth of her children, she had been unable to paint. In her youth she was a very talented artist but pregnancy changed all of that. She longed to paint again and her children, now adults, tried encouraging her, but to no avail. She just didn't feel able to put paint to canvas.

In hypnosis I told her to go back and find the root cause of the problem.

Firstly she went back to a life in fifteenth century Venice, where she was a man and spent all of her life enjoying painting. I asked her if this was where the problem lay. She told me no, but she needed to go back to Venice to understand her original passion for paint and for decorating beautiful things. I told her this was fine, but to now go to the life where the problems started.

She next went back to a life in nineteenth century Paris, where as a young girl she was studying both ballet and painting. She loved both of these art forms, but was feeling very angry and frustrated with her father because, due to some financial difficulties, he was asking her to choose to study only one and to abandon the other.

We then skipped forward a couple of years and I asked her which she chose. She gave a huge sigh and said painting was her first love, so it had to be painting. I asked her if she had made the right choice. She said that she had, because she was now married and pregnant with her first child, and because of this she would have given up the ballet anyway. She said she was feeling very creative now and was actually painting every day.

I instructed her to go to just after the birth of her first child. She became upset and started to cry: I told her to go a bit further forward, where she could recount what had happened without feeling quite so distraught. She told me the baby, a boy, was stillborn and her husband was blaming her for the death. I asked her what had she done? She told me that she had continued to paint right up to the last days of the pregnancy. Her husband was convinced that the baby had died due to all the paint fumes she had inhaled during the nine-month period. She was certain he was right, and also blamed herself. Her husband subsequently left her because of this, so she was grieving not only for the baby, but also for the loss of her husband.

She was holding a deep sense of guilt and really believed the baby's death was all her fault. We needed to clear out all of these negative emotions, so I took her into the spirit world to meet the baby. She asked the child for forgiveness and released the vow she made to never paint again. She then forgave her husband for everything he did to hurt her, and asked him to forgive her as well. She then completely forgave herself for everything that happened. When I brought her back she understood absolutely why she had given up painting when she became pregnant in this lifetime. I am pleased to report that she is now happily painting again.

This is yet another example of someone having no conscious reason for behaving in a certain way. and how hypnosis can bring a problem to the surface and solve it.

Young children are often born with outstanding natural abilities. Society usually calls these children geniuses but could it not be that these kids are carrying this knowledge through from other lifetimes?

When people know that I am a past life regression therapist, the first question asked is usually; how many people have I hypnotised who were well known or famous in other lifetimes? The answer is-very few. However I have often hypnotised people who are witnesses to some event in history, such as the death of Jesus or the burning of Joan of Arc. Again, who am I to say if these were real happenings, or if the person is tapping into the Akashic records and "seeing" the event?

To clarify this a bit further the Akashic records, sometimes called the halls of learning or the cave of creation, are where a complete record of humanity is stored. I see the cave as being crystalline in nature; it represents all humanity on Earth. It is multidimensional, yet it is deeply hidden within the Earth and will never be found.

The Akashic records contain the record of every soul who has ever lived on the Earth plane. There is a crystalline structure for each individual soul, and within that crystal is imprinted a record of all the lifetimes that soul has reincarnated. The crystal holds all the knowledge relating to karma: why souls have chosen the parents they have, both in this and in other lifetimes, their karmic grouping and the challenges and knowledge they have acquired.

We all have our own connection, or pointers, to the Akashic records within our own individual DNA. Our personal DNA stores our own individual Akashic record. Since we are all interconnected and the universe is holographic, people, when they are in hypnosis, are often able to tap into these records and sometimes experience the 'past lives' of others as their own.

There is no problem or judgement should this happen: it is all about learning, and it may help that person in some way to gain a greater realisation of self by connecting with the lifetime of another.

What is important to me because most of my work is about clearing up negative emotions and fear, is how my client is affected by what they are feeling or seeing.

A few years ago I worked with a very young girl who went back to London in the Swinging Sixties. She became a beautiful, glamorous model, who was very much part of the 'in crowd' and the Carnaby Street scene at the time. We went a few months forward and she found herself in Paris. I asked her what she was doing there and all she would say was: "Oh my God, Jimmy is dead. Jimmy is dead." I asked her if Jimmy was her boyfriend and she said "no". I suddenly felt that I knew who Jimmy was but, as I didn't want to put any words into her mouth, I asked her if Jimmy was known just to her, or if he was someone the public would recognise. She said he was well-known as a pop singer.

Jimmy of course turned out to be Jim Morrison of the Doors, an American rock band from the 1960s. I asked her if she knew him well and she said not intimately, but she was part of a group of people he often partied with. I asked her what he was really like and she said: "Oh he was an absolute monster, but I loved him as did everyone else." Then she started to cry.

I then took her forward to a point a bit further on when she, still a beautiful young woman, was killed in a car crash. She told me that she had come back in this lifetime to be more normal and to value life more. In the last lifetime she was careless and abused her body with drugs. Now she had learnt her lesson and was going to be much more respectful and careful in this life.

Diane, another lady I worked with, went back to the reign of King Charles I of England. She had already witnessed various battles scenes before, with another therapist, but the major issues relating to a deep sense of guilt were not dealt with at the time.

She got really upset as she realised what a weak man she was in that lifetime, and was very aware that he could have handled so many situations very differently. As we progressed further into the life she could also see and feel a noose around her neck. Those experiences caused her a sense of deep regret; to the point where she has dedicated this lifetime to always being there for, and helping, other people. When I first met Diane, she was also inclined to apologise to everyone for everything she did. This has improved now that she is standing in her own power, and because the deep sense of guilt she was holding onto for so long has been released.

Sometimes people tune into the lives of famous people. Often, when you ask them to really step back and look, sense and feel the body they are in, their perspective changes, and they are more likely to know or know of the well known person. However if there is deep trauma, or a sense of regret and horror at what the person believes he or she has done, they may well be the reincarnation of some quite infamous person. Whether they are or not, they obviously relate very strongly with that soul, so it is important to deal with all the negative emotions from seeing that lifetime that are brought within them.

Sometimes women feel a deep connection with Mary Magdalene. I have regressed at least three different people who all believe they were Mary. All the lives described were completely different. Now, it is not for me to say who, if any, of these women were correct. However all of them were deeply spiritual people, and probably were part of the Essene faith around the time of Jesus.

The most interesting famous case I worked with was actually just before this book was going into print. Again, this may be that the client was tapping into the Akashic records. However as she was so severely traumatised by the lifetime I am going to describe, I believe that in her case it was an absolutely genuine re-living of one of her past lives.

A very attractive 18 year old girl came to see me in London because she had suddenly felt a very urgent need to experience past life regression. Lucy (not her real name) had a history of depression and anorexia. She was experiencing very vivid dreams where she saw herself dressed in old fashioned clothing, and performing in front of crowds of people. She felt that past life regression would be able to help her to understand more. I took her into hypnosis and suggested that she find the lifetimes she most needed to clear for her to begin to feel better in this life as Lucy.

We went into a couple of past lives which we sorted out and forgave. Then, from a life as a child called Anna who was standing over a tombstone crying over the death of her mother, she instantly flipped into a completely different life. This can sometimes happen. At first I thought she was still in the life of Anna, but then things took a completely different turn.

I always give clients a safety valve; so that any time they are uncomfortable they can lift a hand and automatically go back into their safe place. Or I can take them into an auditorium to watch the scene as a spectator. If something is really traumatic they can be the projectionist, watching themselves watching the film. These are NLP dissociation techniques, and can be very useful anytime the client starts to become distressed.

Lucy began to get very upset and started to cover her face, telling me that she had to get away from the photographers because she couldn't breathe. I told her she was safe, and immediately moved her out of the picture and into the auditorium where she could continue to watch, but without feeling so distraught. She began to calm down and I started to ask her questions.

Liz: (at that time assuming we were still with Anna) How old are you now and why are the photographers there?
Lucy: (still upset and talking in a tiny anxious voice) I am 21. I've made accomplishments. People seem to look up to me but I don't understand. It's like they think I have accomplished something.
Liz: What sort of accomplishment is it that people want to know more about?
Lucy: I've been in the movies.
Liz: OK.
Lucy: My name got changed.
Liz: What did it get changed to?
Lucy: Judy.
Liz: Do you like being in the movies or not?
Lucy: No.
Liz: What do you do in the movies?
Lucy: I do musicals. My mother made me perform. I have been performing so much I never have the time to do anything else.
Liz: So how does all of that make you feel?
Lucy: A sense of love and appreciation to the people who look up to me, but I feel empty. I don't feel loved inside.
Liz: Because you haven't learnt to love yourself have you?
Lucy: No, I am so... tired.
Liz: Because they keep you working all the time?
Lucy: (starting to cry again) They give me prescription drugs to keep me awake.
Liz: Its OK, stay in the auditorium and out of the picture.
Liz: What is your surname? What are they calling you?
Lucy: Garland
Liz: Yes, I thought it might be. So you have been making lots and lots of pictures? The producers keep you performing?

Lucy: (getting upset again) Yes.

Liz: It's OK. This is all about sorting all of this out, so that the person who is now Lucy can move on in her life. What happens next?

Lucy: Everybody must call me Judy because they are told they must obey.

Liz: That's OK. I will call you Judy.

Lucy: Yes, Judy.

Liz: When we last spoke you were 21. Go forward and tell me where you are now.

Lucy: (seeming surprised) Oh, I've got my own show. Liza is with me. She sings with me.

Liz: She is very good isn't she?

Lucy: I love her with all my heart. She's had no life, like me.

Liz: So she went on the stage quite young, did she?

Lucy: (starting to cry again) Yes, I needed to make money; the producers were prodding me to make money. I have no money for the children.

Liz: So they made you put Liza on the stage as well?

At this point she starts crying so much that her words become indecipherable for a while.

Lucy: I just keep having another drink on top of another drink.

Liz: So is that to hide what you are feeling?

Lucy: They all think I am crazy. I am not mad. I just want to be a good mother.

Liz: You have another daughter too don't you?

Lucy: Yes.

Liz: And she is on the stage?

Lucy: No, she is too young.

Liz: So you are trying to look after another child as well, but you have to keep on performing is that right?

Lucy: Yes.

Liz: So you have been married.

Lucy: Yes, I met my husband on the *St Louis* set. He doesn't want me anymore; he says I drink too much.

Liz: It's OK. So where do we need to go now? You are completely safe. This is all about giving you some sort of rest and peace.

Lucy: I'm in my flat in London. I've no direction, no one wants me. I'm so... alone. All of this work for nothing.

Liz: It's OK. You are safe, so what happens next?

Lucy: I got it in my head, the pill; I flushed it down with whisky. I can't take anymore.

Liz: OK, so you are drinking the whisky and taking the pills, is that right?

Lucy: I feel light, but at the same time I am suffocated and trapped.

Liz: It's alright we are here to help you. Is it correct that although you find yourself out of your body, you are still hanging around, Judy?

Lucy: Yes.

Lucy: I was a terrible mother.

Liz: No you weren't. It is OK.

Liz: So what I am going to do now is to ask the Archangel Michael to take you into the spirit world, so that you won't be around feeling guilty any more. Do I have your permission to do that?

Lucy: Yes.

Liz: Alright. I am going to touch Lucy's arm and use Theta Healing to take this lost soul fragment of Judy into the light. Is that alright?

Lucy: Yes.

Liz: I want you to tell me when you feel yourself being lifted up. The angels are holding you in their wings and you are being taken into the light. I want you to tell me when you are in the light.

Lucy: I am in the light.

Liz: I know that you are still feeling guilty towards your children, and as a part of us never leaves the spirit world, and this world is just a projection, what would you like to say to them?

Lucy: I just want them to know to not let themselves be treated like a child. They wouldn't let me grow. I don't want them to go through 22 hours of work a day. I am tired.

Liz: You are going to be fine. Can you forgive yourself for everything that happened in that lifetime as Judy so that you can let it go?

Lucy: Yes.

Liz then talks her through a complete forgiveness sequence.

Liz: So, how do you feel now? Can you let all of this go or is there something else?

Lucy: There is something else.

Liz: What is it? Do you need to forgive the producers or your mother? What is it you need to let go of?

Lucy: My drug addict ways. There is too much intake. I need too much. I need to look after my three children.

Liz: The three children are fine. They are grown up now and are very good at looking after themselves. Go forward and see your children now.

Lucy: Yes, Liza is going to be a star.

Liz: Yes, she is a big star.

Lucy: She is very beautiful.

Liz: So now that you know they are all fine, do you think that you can forgive yourself and let go of the addiction?

Lucy: Yes, I can let go.

Liz goes through a further forgiveness sequence with her.

Liz: Take the hand of the Archangel Michael. How does it feel?

Lucy: Loved.

Once again, we can see that this is not actually about going into a lifetime where a person has lived with fame. It is about resolving all the trauma that was caused, so that the soul as it is now can let go of trauma and move on.

Chapter 14: Letting Go and Cutting Ties

Both powerful and negative emotions can affect us and hold us back in so many ways. These feelings do not necessarily have to be bad – they can just be very strong. Most of us live with a combination of both positive feelings of love for people and places, and old harmful feelings we may or may not be aware we have. Our belief systems frequently stop us clearing away the stuff we no longer want, or need, in our lives. By this I am not necessarily talking about other people and relationships. It can be material objects as well.

For example, a woman may decide to sell her house. She may absolutely love her home, and associates it with a particularly happy time in her life. Now, because her children are grown up and her husband is no longer around, she needs to sell it. She still has such a deep association with the house that her subconscious mind may do everything it can to stop the sale. She may choose a bad estate agent, or a newspaper with a low success rate, to promote the sale. This will not be done consciously by the owner. She will probably become very frustrated when the building fails to sell, but because she is still emotionally tied to it she is unconsciously sabotaging its sale.

I remember a few years ago I worked with a very good friend who has his own garage. He is a mechanic who also buys and sells cars for a living. He is a natural salesman, and anything he decides to sell is quickly snapped up. That is, until he decided to sell his own BMW. He told me that no matter what he did, it just wouldn't sell.

I asked him to tell me about his own history with the car so that we could sort it out and let it go.

He said as a boy he always wanted a dark blue, soft top BMW car. Then when his business became successful he finally managed to buy one, and he and his girlfriend would often put the top down and go on long drives into the country. It was a happy time in his life. Now he was no longer with the girlfriend, the split was acrimonious and she was causing him a lot of trouble. I asked him if he was ready to let go of the car emotionally. He said one of the reasons he now wanted to sell the car was because every time he drove it he could still remember her sitting beside him: the memory of this was making him very angry.

He agreed that perhaps he needed to let go of the emotional ties the car represented to him in order to sell it. I told him to sit down, close his eyes and visualise talking to his car. I suggested that he thank the car for all the happy times it had given him, and to let it know that he was now ready to release it. I told him to then visualise cutting all the cords and ties he has with the car. Once he had done that he was to put it into a pink bubble and to send it away with love. As he thanked the car for all the happy times it gave him, the tears were streaming down his face. He realised that up until that moment he hadn't really wanted to sell the car, but now he was ready to finally let it go. He phoned me later that day to tell me- success- he had just sold the car!

This is just one true example of how we hold on to things and how we sometimes need to release the emotions tying us to these things, so we can move on. When we put a lot of love into caring for something it is often difficult to release it. Houses provide shelter and sanctuary from an often harsh outside world. Being inside them helps us to feel protected and safe, so when we say goodbye to them it is really like having to let go of an old friend. We remember happy times spent with special people, therefore it is hardly surprising we find it difficult to say goodbye.

On many occasions I have seen clients cry when they release a house. They can feel as though they are being asked to let go of a part of themselves. However, although this can be a painful exercise, it does work and can really help people to move on. A house will generally be snapped up very quickly afterwards.

It is the same with our relationships with people. How can you step into a new happy rapport with someone when you are still emotionally and etherically tied to your old partner? They may be someone you have, many lifetimes ago, promised to love for all eternity; a part of you will find it almost impossible to let them go. Your new partner may also be someone you promised to love forever in another lifetime, so you will also feel you have to be with them. Complicated isn't it! This is why it is so important to release everything connected with an old relationship before commencing a new one.

So many things bind us to people and places. It is hardly surprising that people tell me they have been trying to split from their existing partner for years, but even though there are no children involved they just can't seem to let go.

Cutting detrimental attachments

We stay tied to people through anger, regret, resentment, jealousy and many more negative emotions, and also because we have made vows to them. These can be vows of love but they can also be vows of vengeance and hatred. Once we fully understand what is holding us together with someone in a negative way we can release all the oaths and vows and forgive the other person, but more importantly forgive ourselves. Even vows of love can be detrimental and very binding. It is better to just love someone, without doing everything possible to tie that person to us by vowing to love them forever. As evidenced when I worked with Amanda, old peoples homes and hospitals are full of people who really need to move on, but something is still tying them to the earth plane. A part of their mind may already have gone and there may be very little awareness left, but something physical is still keeping them here, tied into this dimension.

So many ties can keep us together, and with the dawning of the internet and mobile phones often these ties are kept up unnecessarily - long after the relationship has finished. Of course we can keep old friends that we see and contact year after year if that feels right to us. Tie cutting is about letting go of old, negative and possibly detrimental attachments.

We have different types of attachments that we sometimes call responsibilities. These include financial attachments and obligations to look after our children, our aged parents and our pets but we also have to know when to let go and allow people to be completely responsible for themselves.

Mothers especially, often find it very difficult to know when to let go of their children. It is important to understand that, by holding on to objects and to people, we are not doing either them or ourselves any favours. We do things to tie people to us in the hope they will stay with us forever, but this is not a good thing either for them or for us. It just makes it more difficult to break free when the time is right and, after all, if you both truly want to stay together it will happen anyway.

Every time we are in contact, or touch a person, we are creating a connection with them. We have hundreds of ties connecting us to our families and friends. We also have hundreds of other connections we are probably totally unaware of, but certainly don't need. If you work as a healer, or someone who deals with deep social problems, it is especially important to keep doing tie-cutting exercises. Clients are often in a very needy state and will completely drain a therapist's energy if they allow it to happen. I am not in any way saying that this is the client's intention: most are usually completely unaware of what they are doing.

I try to remember to put myself in a bubble of protective light before I see anyone, as this makes me stronger. I also ask for help from the ascended masters and beings of light so that the session is perfect for the client. I also try to remember to tie cut twice every day. So many of the people who come to see me are in deeply troubled emotional states, and I would not be helping them or myself if I held onto their emotional baggage.

Energy stealing

People steal our energy all the time. How many times have you woken up in the morning feeling good only to receive a telephone call from a family member or friend that leaves you feeling completely worn-out? This can happen, especially when the person phones you to say what a terrible time they are having. The more you listen to them the more fatigued you begin to feel, and the better they feel because they are taking all that energy from you.

This can also happen in supermarkets, stations and other places where there are lots of people. You arrive feeling fine, and a few minutes later you start to feel angry and agitated for no apparent reason. When this happens you are tapping into the general negative energy within the place, and also giving up your energy to it.

Protection is something that is talked about a lot, and putting yourself in a bubble can certainly help. However, how often are we in a hurry and forget to do all of the protection exercises we are taught? To some extent I also believe that we are protected at all times whatever we do, but at the same time I know we can also be vulnerable and energetically open. It is also our fears that let us tap into negative emotions we really don't need.

Etheric ties are dangerous to our mental and physical well being. Hawaiians, who use many forms of healing, frequently make it a practice to cut etheric cords, or aka cords as they call them, at least twice a day.

One way to do this is to sit in a meditative state, and to ask to be shown all the ties that are in any way attaching you to other people. I often see myself standing in a circle in a safe place: I then ask to be shown another circle, full of the people and objects I need to cut ties from. I may just see people in the other circle, or I may just see lots of ties coming towards me from it. Next I see myself gathering up all of these ties and binding them together – a bit like long hair being put into a pony tail. Then I mentally take a sword and I cut the ties all the way through both from the top and from the bottom.

As I am doing this I ask forgiveness of anyone I have hurt. I forgive anything anyone may have done to hurt me, and I forgive myself for anything I may have done to hurt myself. I then watch the ties dropping away from me and from whoever is in the circle in front of me. Sometimes I have to see myself pulling out the ties and burning them. After all of this is done I make the circle in front of me into a bubble, and send it all away from me to the light, with love. Never underestimate how powerful this exercise can be as it can bring on a real feeling of liberation.

We can also pick up psychic hooks from other people. This can happen when people are jealous of us, and also when a family member is particularly needy. We let people put psychic hooks into us all the time especially when we have feelings of love for that other person. If you become aware of a psychic hook it is a good idea to ask your guides to remove it, and to send it up into the light. Sometimes this can also be a soul fragment of another person. You may also recognise who this fragment belongs to. Again ask for the light workers to remove, cleanse and send this soul fragment either into the light, or to give it back to the person from whence it came, if this is what is needed and is in that person's best interest. I just ask that it be cleansed and sent to where it needs to go. I trust that this will be done. I also do a three-way forgiveness between myself and the other person so we become more emotionally free of one another.

Hooponopono (see Chapter 11 for further information) is a really good way for this clearing work to be done properly. It is a process that involves freeing and forgiving yourself, to make everything that is brought into your life well. I can say from personal experience it is a fantastic healing method that really works.

Chapter 15: Chakras

Many healers work by focusing on the physical and energetic centres of the body. This can be done using many different techniques and is again about clearing and creating flow. These energy centres are known as Chakras – a word derived from the ancient Sanskrit word meaning wheel. The Chakras are not visible to the naked eye, but can be clearly seen by people with clairvoyant ability. We have seven Chakras in our bodies, each a different colour and spinning, with further Chakras beneath our feet and above our heads, connecting us to the universe.

There is a new Chakra appearing between the heart and throat Chakras, although not everyone seems to have it or perhaps it is not yet open in everyone. The heart Chakra is generally recognised as being green with sometimes pink showing, and the throat Chakra is blue; the new Chakra is turquoise. These Chakras are important because they connect us with other dimensions and realities. Many healers can feel when a person's Chakras are out of balance. They can feel when they are blocked and not spinning as they should. They also know when negative entities are trapped within them. They use their hands to clear out whatever needs to go. One of the best books I have read explaining about the Chakras is by Barbara Ann Brennan, and is called *Hands of light*.

Cleaning and clearing

As a hypnotherapist, I often use a simple method of asking the client to visualise walking into different coloured rooms. Each room symbolises a different Chakra. I tell the client that each of these rooms has to be perfectly balanced for them. Therefore each room will need to be light, airy, clean and exactly as it has to be for their perfect well being. I'll have a good understanding of what is going on with them emotionally so I will know which rooms they will find the most challenging to clear up.

We start with the base Chakra, which is red. This Chakra represents grounding and controls our connection to the earth. It is linked with our self preservation and survival instincts. The more grounded we are the more we are able to function on the earth plane and the more safe and secure we feel.

After I have instructed the client to go into the red room, I ask them to describe it to me. Obviously everyone's description is different, but we work through whatever needs to be done to make the room perfect. They may want to open the windows or give the room a good clean. The furnishings may have to be changed or all the old clutter cleared away. When they have finished, and the room is perfect, they then come out and close the door behind them before moving into the next room. The main thing is that they end up with bright airy rooms and bright spinning Chakras. I work through this whole exercise going from red into the orange room, then into all the other rooms, finishing with the crown Chakra, which is usually seen as a silvery violet colour.

Of course all of this is symbolic, but since it is all done with the correct intent the client's Chakras are perfectly balanced after this exercise.

One thing I have noted, as I go through this procedure with different people, is that they will sometimes say to me that in the magenta (or third eye) room there is a big cross blocking off the light. If this had only happened once I would have probably dismissed it, but I have now been told this by many different people on separate occasions.

The first time this happened I didn't really get the significance of it until I asked a client where the cross came from, and why was it blocking the light? He told me the priest had put it there when he was a baby, to stop him remembering his true connection with his higher self and with God. I asked him when the priest had put it there. He said it happened when he was baptised, and it was one of the ways the church uses to control its subjects by stopping them connecting with their true intuitive selves. The church wants him to understand the reality of God as portrayed by them. If he stayed open and therefore clairvoyant, in all probability he would not become a follower and the church would have no control over his mind. Therefore the church tried to stop these natural abilities in any way it could. This rather surprised me, but I have been told the same thing about baptism so many times now that I certainly see it as a possibility. Especially as, once the cross is removed from the third eye, the person's clairvoyant abilities seem to improve.

It appears to me that a lot of wires have become crossed here. Since the original idea of baptism was a cleansing done in water, the sign of the cross would never have been used. Baptisms are more associated with John the Baptist, and the cross became a symbol of Christianity only after the death of Jesus. So, who knows? In my experience if a baby is baptised, it seems to close the third eye.

The cross is actually a very interesting symbol. When we make the sign of the cross in front of our body we are actually opening up our auric field to outside influences. This can make us more vulnerable, more defenceless and more susceptible to outside suggestion. The same thing happens when we salute someone, which is why military bodies use it at all times.

Simple muscle testing using kinesiology can prove this to be the case. Anything that potentially messes with our auric field can affect us both physically and mentally. While making the sign of the cross does not have a long lasting effect, it does make us more susceptible to other people's suggestions.

Chapter 16: Theta Healing

We are being told again and again how we create our own reality. Books such as *The Secret* and *What the Bleep* have changed the way we view our world, and help us to understand that we are not actually victims of circumstance. We are told that we have to keep making positive affirmations so that everything in our life will change in a positive way. Yes of course all of this is possible. However, what is so often not explained is that unless we change our core negative beliefs about ourselves it will be extremely difficult to create this wonderful, fulfilling future we all dream about.

Core beliefs

What is a core belief? A core belief is something we believe about ourselves on a very deep level. It is a knowledge we hold within us that we are probably completely unaware of because it is locked in our unconscious mind. So, on a conscious level we may think that we are worthy and capable of doing whatever we want to do, but on a subconscious level we know that we are worthless and unable to achieve anything. This then creates a deep conflict within us that often stops us from doing anything at all.

Where do these deep core beliefs come from? Well, often from our childhood, but also from past or parallel lives. It is important to understand that a child up to the age of about seven years old continuously fluctuates between alpha and theta brainwaves. So a young child is continually in hypnosis. This means they are completely open to all types of suggestions: both positive and negative.

When people go to a hypnotherapist to feel better about themselves, they will hear all sorts of positive suggestions to help them do so. Children cannot choose what they hear so they just absorb everything. This is fine if they are told they are clever, beautiful, handsome, worthy, happy, how much they are loved and how safe they are. Children, however, are more often told they are a nuisance, hopeless and other derogatory words by parents, teachers, priests, other adults and even their own friends. Children copy from adults, so they repeat what they hear back to other children. They also pick up negative messages from TV and the media.

I remember being told as a young child that I was hopeless at maths and would always be so; that I needed a fringe because I looked funny without one; how unfortunate it was that I had inherited my father's slightly prominent chin, and what a pity I had my mother's eyes because my father's would have made me look much better. These are the ones I remember, but I am sure there were many more. These things were not said with any particular malice, more as a matter of fact; as a result I grew up believing them to be true. I was brought up in a happy loving home, but what about all the children who grew up believing they were completely worthless and unlovable because of what they were told. These things stay with us for life or in some cases lifetimes.

We create these core beliefs within our children, and as a result we take their confidence away. Therefore, if someone who is generally considered to be bright keeps failing entrance exams, it is important to find out what they really believe on a deeper level. They may feel that they are not worthy to go to university, or that they will be setting themselves up for failure. Once the core belief is removed the person is free to move forward in a much more positive way.

Dual beliefs

We hold so many core beliefs, and it is important to find out what it is that is stopping us from being who we really want to be. We often hold dual beliefs that conflict with one another. For example, we may believe that we are clever but at the same time believe that we are stupid. We may know that we can achieve many things, but also feel that we are useless and won't be able to get anywhere. Most of this is going on in our subconscious mind; therefore we are constantly in conflict with ourselves and our beliefs without knowing and understanding what is really going on within us. This can very easily create a sort of elastic band effect. We go forward a bit and then we are pulled back again without realising why all this is happening.

Theta Healing was created by Vianna Stibal (www.thetahealing. com). She managed to cure herself of cancer by using the theta brainwave to visualise herself travelling up through many different dimensions, and connecting with the energy of all creation, or God. Whilst in this altered consciousness she watched the cancer in her body disappearing. When she returned to her conscious state and became fully aware of her physical body, her cancer had gone and she was completely healed. She then realised that she could do the same for other people, and started to get amazing results by curing people of various diseases. After working like this for a while, she realised that people were bringing their illnesses back. So she used Theta Healing to ask why. The message she received was that people's core beliefs were bringing the illnesses back. She needed to remove the core negative beliefs from the person so that they would not only get better but they would stay cured. If for example, someone believed that they were unworthy to be alive, they would create an illness that would in effect kill them. We have thousands of core beliefs so it is important to completely clear out as many of the really negative ones as we can.

What Vianna realised was that the more questions she asked the nearer she got to the core belief, and the more she fed the answer back to the person the nearer she got to the answer. For example, if someone is very afraid of being left by their partner she would ask: "What would be the worst thing that can happen to you if your partner leaves you?" The answer is usually something to do with being left on their own. Vianna then asks: "What will be the worst thing that can happen to you if you are left on your own?" and they reply that they would be lonely. She would then ask: "What is the worst thing that can happen to you if you are lonely?" This line of questioning goes on until she gets right down to the root of the problem. This is usually when the client just keeps repeating the same answer, which can be something like: "I am unlovable. I am undeserving. I've been abandoned by God," or "I am unworthy". Vianna then uses Theta Healing to visualise pulling out the negative belief and to reinstate a positive version of the same.

This work is very powerful and can clear up no end of old problems, whilst creating a positive space and enabling the person to move forward. Illnesses disappear and people's approaches to life become much more positive.

Chapter 17: Shifting Negative to Positive

Affirmations can be an excellent way of focusing the mind and if you truly believe what you are saying they will work; just as long as you don't have any core beliefs that are opposing them.

Noah St. John (www.afformations.com/main.php) recognised the subconscious mind's need to answer questions, so he invented afformations. This is a means of asking yourself positive questions such as: "Why is my life so perfect now?" "Why am I my perfect weight now?" This way, your subconscious mind has to find the answer and show you why your life is so great now! Therefore, by using the words 'why' and 'now' affirmations become far more powerful.

We can take all this much further and look into the belief systems we have been holding on to from past lives. In theory, once one life is over that part of us should be integrated with the 'over soul', and we are then ready to move on to the next life. However, there is so much that can keep us earthbound. Therefore if we are angry, and have unresolved issues from a past life, that part of us is not integrated with the rest of our soul. This is why we make the same mistakes again and again, and why we often carry anger and phobias from a past lifetime.

My belief is probably not the same as many past life therapists. I believe that if a person is shown one of their past lives, it is because there is something as yet unresolved in that lifetime. This usually means total and absolute forgiveness of self is what is needed, also forgiveness of other people, and rescinding and releasing all oaths, vows, promises, contracts and sometimes curses. Once this is done the soul part can be reintegrated, and whatever is causing the illness, phobia or problem in this lifetime can all be let go. Therefore all the belief systems change in that lifetime, causing them to also change in this.

When I first began to understand about core beliefs and started to clear them my life changed dramatically for the better. Now I understand that, if I feel stuck in any way, I have to go to the root cause of the problem and clear up all of the core beliefs that are blocking me in some way. I change all the negative beliefs into positive ones and the blockage miraculously goes away.

Fear creates many blockages and it is always important to get to the root cause of the fear so that it can be eliminated. We often buy into other people's fears and that is never a good thing to do. When I work with very fearful people I often get them to tune into their body to find out where they feel the fear. If there is a spirit attachment in that area I first remove it, and then I ask the client to tune into the fear.

One of the ways to do this is by telling them to spin back in time, right back to the root cause of the problem, whilst still allowing them to feel the fear. I then tell them to let a picture come into their mind and to look down at their feet and to see what kind of body they are in. Are they in their body or are they in a different body? We lock so much fear in our bodies so it is important to find out where it is and let it all go. The more we work on ourselves to clear out negative energy and memories the better we feel about ourselves, and the more ready we are to step into a positive and creative reality.

Negative beliefs and relationships

Relationships mirror the negative as well as the positive feelings we have about ourselves. Therefore the more work we do to clear out the negative core beliefs the less likely we are to attract a partner who will treat us badly. If we hold beliefs that we deserve to be treated badly, to be abandoned, or to be verbally or physically abused then that is exactly the sort of partner we will attract. Once we change these core beliefs this will no longer happen.

Partnerships fall apart because people are changing all the time. This is why, when one half of a couple starts to work deeply on themselves, that relationship often falls completely apart. The person doing the work realises that they are no longer prepared to put up with the way things are. Often the other half is given an ultimatum. At this point it is up to the partner to either accept the new person they are living with and to change accordingly, or to find themselves left behind.

It may be hard to accept that our love life is governed by the issues we need to clear within ourselves. At the same time, if we truly believe that we deserve to be in a very loving and supportive relationship that is also what we will attract. So it does work both ways.

When we are in an abusive relationship, whether this is physical or mental, it is important to work on ourselves to find out the belief system that is attracting this. Theta Healing is one powerful way of doing this, or alternatively we can use hypnosis to release it. Frequently I use a combination of both methods while at the same time working on the forgiveness and clearing of all the negative oaths and vows. Of course abusive relationships are not just between married couples. They can be between father and daughter, mother and daughter, father and son, daughter and stepfather, brother and sister, stepbrother and stepsister, son and uncle etc.

With so many marriages and relationships breaking up at the moment we constantly have to deal with new challenges. Children find themselves having to live with new stepmothers and fathers as well as new siblings. Of course nothing is ever by chance; often there are big past life issues to be resolved within these families.

Sometimes it can be extremely difficult for a parent bringing their children from a previous relationship into a new marriage. The children and the stepparent will hopefully get on, but sometimes they will dislike one another intensely. It is also the same when children find themselves expected to love and get on with new siblings. All of this is very tricky to deal with especially when no one really understands what is going on.

I recently worked with a married couple: the stepfather disliked one of his stepsons from the moment he met him. However, because he loved his new wife-to-be, he still went ahead with the marriage. She soon found herself not only in the role of wife but also that of peacemaker. Also she just couldn't understand why her husband constantly criticised one of her sons, and also why that particular son hated his new stepfather on sight.

The boy had never really known his real father, who died of alcoholism when he was a baby; he kept saying he did want his mother to be happy, but not with 'Him' as he called his stepfather. The new husband did try for the sake of his wife to be a father to the boy but found it extremely difficult to hide his dislike of him. Interestingly he experienced no such problems with the other son, who he loved instantly.

When I regressed the father we found that the stepson he disliked so intensely had killed him in many lifetimes. The soul fragments from those lifetimes were still hanging around on the earth plane and they were very angry at having been killed.

The first thing we did was to visualise bringing those soul fragments into the light. Once these parts of the client became aware of the higher vibration, they could be healed and forgive the perpetrator of the crime.

We worked through two different lifetimes, and then he said that all the anger and frustration he felt towards the boy was gone. He also asked forgiveness of the boy's higher self and asked that the relationship between them be finally healed. He started to cry and told me that he knew that he could now finally love the boy, and be the father to him that he so desperately wanted to be.

This was a great result for me because the outcome of that session really affected the whole family in such a positive way.

Abuse so often happens when there are step-parents involved because there are often strong past life issues to be resolved between these individuals. If, for example, the stepfather had some sort of relationship with the daughter in a past life he will probably still be attracted to her in some way. His knowing that he is not a blood relative sometimes makes the situation excusable in his own mind, and he will push the boundaries further than he knows he should. The wife may, on some level, be aware of his feelings for the daughter and this will bring up all her insecurities about herself. She may even begin to resent her daughter as well as her husband, because the daughter is becoming a beautiful young woman while she herself is rapidly ageing and losing her looks.

All of this may be very subtle and on a conscious level no one is really aware of what is going on, but it can lead to dangerous undercurrents. The stepfather may hug the daughter just a little too tight, and the daughter can feel scared of someone who is masquerading as her father. The daughter usually sees the stepfather as a dirty old man, and cannot possibly understand why he is making advances to her. He equally cannot understand her rejection of him. The husband may also not understand why he is attracted to two women at the same time, and so it goes on.

This is just one possible scenario and there are many different combinations. All of them are interesting from a therapist's point of view, but not so enjoyable for the people living through them.

When I work with these scenarios I nearly always come across oaths and vows that require releasing and rescinding. Hence I always clear all of these; together with the forgiveness that is a prerequisite of this kind of therapy. When we think of all the past lives we are still experiencing it is hardly surprising how many oaths and vows we need to clear. For example, just imagine that you have taken the marriage vows in most of your previous lives. Yes, we do meet the same souls again and again, but we also interact with them in many different ways. How many times have you told different souls that you would love them forever? Therefore, just think how many etheric ties are still binding between you and these other people.

In the example given above, once all the old oaths and vows are released between the stepfather and stepdaughter, the situation between them will definitely change in some way. The father usually finds that any attraction he felt to the daughter will just fade away, and he starts to treat her as a proper daughter, or circumstances will change and the daughter may go away to school or college. The main thing that happens is that a very dangerous situation is defused and the wife starts to get her husband back.

Of course some stepfather and daughter situations can be very different. The stepdaughter can be the child the stepfather always wanted, and by marrying the child's mother the man walks into a ready-made family, but it doesn't always happen like that.

If only we can begin to understand that, when we are presented with a problem, it is our higher self's way of making us clear it up and sort it. We will feel much more in control of our lives, and we will have the knowledge that we can change anything by just making a conscious effort to do it.

Chapter 18: Decisions and Gratitude

How often do you feel stuck and depressed in relation to a situation, or just about life in general? Your life is going badly and there seems to be no way out. Then suddenly the phone will ring and someone will ask you to go on holiday with them, or a new contract will suddenly come in. Everything changes in an instant and suddenly the world looks a very different place. We all know that feeling, and know how different we feel once we have new hope.

So often when people feel depressed they just give up. They give into the negative feelings, and they hand their power for recovery over to a doctor who just gives them a prescription for antidepressants. These pills make them feel groggy and disassociated from their feelings: they just continue to plough on day to day without really getting any worse, but not getting any better either. They no longer feel in charge of their life, and it is as if they are on the outside looking in at themselves. When they have finished the pills they go back to the doctor who just gives them some more tablets, and so it may go on for years and years.

What is important for everyone to realise is that, when things are going badly for us, it should not be about giving up. It should be about deciding what it is that is creating this deep dissatisfaction and how the situation can be changed. Often, just by making a conscious decision to look into new ways to improve our lives, new opportunities come up.

Over the years scientists have tried to find out what makes people happy. It cannot be money, because, if that is the case, why are so many people who have much material wealth so unhappy?

Most research points to looking into what you enjoy doing best, and then finding a way to bring pleasure to other people by doing it: for example, if you are a talented musician and really enjoy playing the piano. By playing the piano for other people you will feel fulfilled by what you are doing, whilst at the same time you are giving enjoyment to your audience.

This can be something even simpler, such as a grandmother really loving it when her grandchildren come to stay. She cooks them all their favourite foods and encourages them to play their favourite games. The grandmother is happy and fulfilled because they are with her, and the same with the children.

Self-concordant goals

The best way to view this is by looking inwards and finding what you really enjoy doing. This is called creating a self-concordant goal, which really means finding something to do that truly reflects your own interests and values.

In my own case it was about learning as much as I could about hypnosis, past life regression, CBT, EFT, soul retrieval, spirit release, NLP, Theta Healing, etc. Then qualifying in these therapies so that I could be doing something I really enjoy, whilst helping other people and getting paid for it. When we continue doing jobs we find boring, or that we dislike, we are not fulfilling our soul's purpose. We are just sitting on the fence, afraid to go either forward or backwards, and we are probably miserable most of the time.

When our self-concordant goal is coupled with something that can also help mankind in some way, this can be called having an intrinsic goal. For example, a man may want to study medicine and that is his self-concordant goal. Once he qualifies and actually practises as a doctor he will also have arrived at his intrinsic goal, or his true calling, which is to heal people. He is doing a job he loves but he is also giving to the world. According to the experts, this is definitely the best way to find true happiness. I know that I love what I am doing, and it also feels great when people leave my office feeling healed. Therefore, the answer seems to be to take the first step towards doing what you really enjoy , looking into how you can bring pleasure, or help other people by what you do; consequently everything else will just come together.

One small change

Often it is about making just one small change and then tweaking it a bit more and a bit more until everything just opens up in the way we really want it to. This may be something simple, like making a decision to join an evening class or just taking an internet correspondence course, or you might want to join a club or a discussion group. Whatever it is, bear in mind that this is all about making a conscious decision to change something in your life, and about actually doing it now.

Remember, whoever said procrastination is the thief of time was correct. Don't just keep putting something off because you are either lazy, or afraid. If you get into this pattern you will persist in making excuses and continue procrastinating. The end result will then be doing nothing, because either you will have forgotten what your original intention was, or you will have talked yourself into why it will not work.

When I left Italy I made my decision to leave almost instantly. I knew I was no longer happy with my job and my partner. I had the option either to continue to feel miserable, or to change my life. When I made the decision to go I left in less than a week. I sorted out everything from England once I was settled there. That is a choice I have never regretted making: I was not happy or fulfilled anymore so I changed everything about my life.

Often creating change can be a daunting experience. Every fear in the book can bubble to the surface in a really terrifying way. My returning to England meant that, after 19 years with a partner in my life, I was suddenly alone. We shared a business together so when I left him I also left the business to him. I had to get used to English customs again. The way people thought about things and the way they led their lives was so very different from the Italian laid back attitude. Priorities were also very different and it took some getting used to. I just had to go for it, and that is what I did.

I started with sales because that was something I knew I could do well, and then I went on to become a court interpreter in an international fraud case, which then lead me to other court interpreting work. I didn't like either of these jobs much, but I needed to keep tweaking until I found what I wanted and felt fulfilled to do. I also met a lawyer, who became a really good friend and a great help to me later when I was looking for premises in Harley St, London.

Sometimes it is also about taking the plunge and seeing where it leads. I remember when I went to college I was not thinking about teaching at all, but the tutor would sometimes ask me to work with some of the groups on days when she was really busy. In order to continue do this she told me I would need to take the instructor training course also available at the college. Subsequently, I went on to become a qualified teacher. This later led me to teach Theta Healing and my own courses. I couldn't have dreamt of doing all of this when I first attended the college.

So, decisions are important. Being complacent doesn't bring happiness; it just brings more and more of the same dull, humdrum existence. We need to learn to open up, to change at all times, and to understand when something is not working in our world that we can keep making little changes, until everything is going the way we want it. We must decide what we want and go for it, and also trust that all will be well. If something doesn't work out, then never mind, we must just think again and take new action. I have often started a project believing it is leading in one direction only to find it takes a completely different course, but actually works out far better than my original plan. Complacency is never an option as far as most successful people are concerned. If something is not working for them they just look for ways to change the situation.

Practising gratitude

Some time ago I met a healer who always practised gratitude. I hadn't heard of this way of working before, but she said when she was feeling down she would do forty minutes of gratitude a day. She explained to me that this just entailed sitting in a relaxed state and saying out loud all the things she was grateful for.

I must admit that I was slightly sceptical, and I also wasn't sure if I could be grateful for that length of time, However I gave it a try, and the more I said different things I was grateful for, the more things I found I actually was really thankful for. This can be anything from the support of my family, having so many friends, living in a country where it is safe to walk alone in a street, or waking up every day feeling healthy. The list is actually endless, and the more you do this exercise the more things you actually become grateful for. It is also about really appreciating what you already have.

Being grateful is a good blues buster. If you are feeling particularly fed up just do forty minutes of being grateful for a few days, and you will suddenly find yourself feeling much better. When we become aware of how much we have to be grateful for, and how little we really do have to moan about, we are ready to make changes.

I recently came across a book called *Thanks!* by Dr Robert Emmons. This paperback is full of interesting points about how our lives can change when we practise gratitude. Dr Emmons, who is a professor at the University of California, tells us that people who regularly practise grateful thinking can increase their happiness levels by as much as twenty five per cent. He also says that keeping a gratitude journal for as little as three weeks can result in better sleep and more energy.

Our health improves, and our attitude becomes far more positive much faster, so it is definitely worth a try and it works for me.

Chapter 19: Animals

The same animals come back to us time and time again. Often they take on our pain and help us cope with our most difficult challenges. When I was a child I just loved going to my grandmother's farm where over the years there were many farm dogs. I loved them all to distraction and spent many happy hours talking to them and playing with them. They always understood me completely, often when grown ups did not. I have always felt a deep affinity with animals, especially with dogs and bears: my idea of heaven is to always have a dog by my side. When my grandmother died she left the farm to my mother and her two sisters. My mother disliked farm life so she quickly sold her share to her two sisters. It was a big house and easily divided up to make two large separate wings. The two sisters continued to share the house for many years until the older, unmarried one died.

At one time my mother's younger sister, my Auntie Peg, had a collie dog called Bosun. My uncle was a Navy man and my aunt had served in the Wrens, hence the choice of name. Bosun was an incredibly intelligent sheepdog, who took his responsibilities very seriously, and would effortlessly round up sheep, cattle or do just about anything he was asked. I remember when he was about three months old and we were walking together: he suddenly decided to demonstrate to me how he was a real sheep dog! He looked at me and then off he went to the far corner of the field where there happened to be about twelve sheep. He then proceeded to round them up and bring them to the gate where I was standing. Of course he was very pleased with himself, and I praised him highly for his ability. Many years later when Bosun died, both my uncle and aunt were very upset. Of all the dogs he was really special.

The year 2003 was a particularly difficult one for my aunt and uncle because their younger son, Warwick, was diagnosed with non-Hodgkins lymphoma. I offered to do some work with him. My guides told me he would not recover, but I could use my abilities to help him release old negative emotions and that was all. I was happy to do what I could. I knew that this was his choice and I understood that his work on Earth was coming to an end. I also knew he would pass between August and September of the following year. I did tell my mother who immediately accused me of being negative, but as far as everyone else was concerned I kept this information to myself and hoped it was wrong; but it wasn't.

My aunt and uncle were, of course, devastated by his illness and naturally always hoped he would recover. This was also an upsetting time for the rest of the family, myself included, as I always felt that he was more like my brother than my cousin. As children, with my brother Richard and his brother Tim, we spent many happy times together. He was the youngest, so how could he go first? Understandably, we all found this difficult to come to terms with.

I think I actually began to know and love the man even more after his death. At his funeral the church, and the gallery above, were full to bursting and people were even standing in the aisles. He dedicated his life to helping people in a quiet unobtrusive way that I, like most people, knew nothing about until after the funeral when everyone came to pay their respects to him. One example of this was being the eyes for his blind friend, and taking him out for long tandem bike rides at least once a week, come rain or come shine. All of the people he helped in so many different ways were there to say thank you, and to pay their last respects to him on that day. I am very proud to say he was my cousin.

At the end of June, six weeks before Warwick's death, a male puppy that was about eight weeks old, seemingly from nowhere, appeared at the farm. He was a tiny little thing, possibly a collie crossed with something else, looking appealingly up at you through one blue and one brown eye. Hungry, wet and bedraggled he was found howling not far from the back door. The moment my aunt and uncle saw him it was love at first sight, and he knew he was back home. Instantly demanding their full attention, once fed and cleaned up, he was ready to play. The older dog Bess, just did not know what to make of him so she either ignored him or treated him with disdain. However he just kept wearing her down until she finally accepted him. They became firm friends and remained so, up to the time of Bess' death.

The moment I heard about this puppy I knew it was Bosun, come back to help them through this difficult time. My guides confirmed this to me and I told my aunt. The interesting thing was that this puppy, or Bosun as he became known, knew his way around the farm from the day he arrived. Even my uncle who has never believed in what he calls "all this esoteric stuff" could not understand how the dog always knew where to go. Little Bosun would just stop and turn around whenever he got to one of the farm's boundaries, just as the old Bosun would have done. All the fields look the same, but he knows exactly where his farm ends from every angle.

The death of Warwick was of course a terrible blow to them, and to all of us, but Bosun did his best to keep them as occupied as possible during that distressing time. This is a classic example of an animal being there to help people through testing times. They would not have got a new dog at that time, so he just had to appear, bringing all that love and playfulness with him.

When my friend Gillian's husband Wally died, their two Bernese dogs, Oban and Ragnar, took on so much of her suffering. These two dogs stayed by her side day and night to give her the strength to carry on. They took on as much of her pain as they could physically cope with. Her heart was so broken that Oban died of a heart attack. Ragnar picked up on her total sense of desperation and developed cancer. They were both young dogs who went well before their time, but their devotion allowed her to work through, and taught her to cope, with her loss. She now has two more Bernese Mountain dogs who are her constant companions.

Dogs always find their right owner. During the nineteen years I lived in southern Italy I often took in, and looked after, many stray dogs and cats that roamed wild in the area. One day a very big, very beautiful, amber coated dog found me, and looked at me with deep soulful, amber eyes. She was very thin, obviously hungry and she had a nasty gash down her left side. I loved her the moment I saw her and knew she was totally mine; I called her Bella, the Italian word for beautiful. She also decided that I was her owner and that was the end of it. I started by feeding her, taking her for long walks and keeping her outside in a kennel at the back of my flat. The climate in that part of Italy is very temperate, and because my flat was small and she was huge, I didn't really have any alternative. Bella had other ideas, and decided to move in with me. She loved travelling by car, and would sit up in the front seat next to me whenever we were going along country roads to the beach. She loved swimming so we would go for miles along the seashore with her diving into the water at every opportunity. I remember how long she took to dry because her coat was so thick and fleecy, and how often my car smelled of wet dog! Neither of us minded.

One day I thought she had been stolen, although I knew that this was impossible as I had left her in the apartment with my mother, who was holidaying with me at the time. It was August, the place was teaming with tourists, and it was far too hot for me to take Bella with me in the car while I went shopping.

Suddenly I saw a dog exactly the same as Bella in someone else's car. My first instinct was panic but then, as I realised she was safe at home, it dawned on me that perhaps she held some sort of pedigree. In those days we had no internet, so I had to find out in other ways. I discovered she was an Italian mountain dog called a Pastore Maremano Abruzzese, or Maremma Sheepdog in English. These dogs are massive, usually pure white, but are also sometimes ivory, orange or a sort of lemony colour. Their eyes are circled in black. Bella was pure orange with beautiful amber eyes that looked as if she was wearing black eyeliner. She was an absolute beauty, highly intelligent and a pedigree!

Bella was with me for about thirteen years in total. She was probably about two years old when I found her, or should I say when she found me. I was distraught when she died and felt as if my world had ended with her. Southern Italians can be horribly cruel to animals, but it never fails to amaze me how someone could abandon such a beautiful and loving creature.

After Bella passed, my cat -a kitten that I had again rescued many years before - also died, and although I was still looking after and helping as many stray animals as I could, nothing would ever be the same again. Also I was ready to leave the personal relationship I was in, and realised it was time to recognise that the universe was telling me I needed to move on. Animals come into our lives for many reasons; to be our companions and to help us. However when they leave us, especially all of them at more or less the same time, it is also time for us to recognise that we too need to shift and move on in some way. I know Bella is still with me. Mediums and clairvoyants I have encountered since I left Italy frequently tell me there is a big dog with me, so Bella never really left. She is just in a different dimension.

Chapter 20: Finding the Light

When I began this work I was guided to call my website Awakening2hypnosis.com. I was aware that people would be almost asleep and in the theta brain wave when I worked with them, but the name made absolute sense to me and still does. Regression hypnosis is a means to awaken people's minds to their true potential.

This work is a long journey of discovery, and a way of awakening ourselves to absolute light or to the freedom the light gives us. The sun is the most powerful energy on our planet. Without it everything would instantly wither and die. It is pure absolute radiance. Therefore, by letting go of all of the darkness within and connecting with the luminosity, and the true brightness that is our higher self, we can finally become liberated.

The world used to be quite a dark and depressing place for me, and now I understand how I was creating that reality for myself. Now I wake in the mornings with a sense of wonder and anticipation as to how each exciting day is going to evolve into a fantastic new adventure in my life.

Travelling all over the world, which I love, allows me to meet many fascinating and diverse people. The places I visit are stunning. America, including the islands of Hawaii, is one of my favourites, as is Rome and other parts of Italy. Europe has many amazingly beautiful places and I am fortunate to have seen many of them.

I have also been to Central America, the Far East, Egypt and the Caribbean.

I also have great freedom of choice to work as and when I wish to, and to teach when I feel inspired to do so. I believe that the clients I attract I am meant to work with, and each and every one of them is interesting and completely different in their own way.

Clients contact me from all over the world, and whether they fly me out to work with them, or whether we do telephone hypnosis, the work is always fascinating. I still have my Harley St. practice in London, and I also work with clients in Bristol.

My vocation is all about teaching people freedom of self-expression. We do not need to be trapped within a given situation, and we always have choices. We make our boundaries by our own limiting beliefs, therefore the moment we recognise that no one else but ourselves can impose restrictions in our lives, we become enlightened. We are free to create, and liberated to attract whatever it is we truly want in our lives.

When people phone me up and tell me they feel stuck it is not me who moves them on - they do that themselves. I am just a facilitator to allow them to let go of all forms of darkness and anger, which then in turn enables them to step into their own chosen version of reality and freedom. I just try to show them how they can find a way to live their lives free from pain and free from depression.

Past life regression and the other treatments I do are never about me as a healer, although the more work I do the more I learn how to expand my own consciousness. My work is all about empowering the other person to grow and to help them get from life whatever it is they really want.

Who knows where my work will take me next. As I am writing this it is April, the sun is shining and I am once again back in Virginia at the invitation of a group of people who have become my friends. Sitting on the porch of an old colonial style Inn surrounded by trees of many colours, pink cherry blossom and others that are every shade of green, violet or white, I am looking at the Blue Ridge Mountains. These are some of the oldest mountains on the planet, and I am thinking how very fortunate I am, once again, to be in these totally beautiful surroundings. There is a very special and unique energy in this area and I absolutely love it.

This evening I am moving to stay with my friend Judy for about a week. She has a beautiful farm in the Virginia countryside and eight very different dogs. So I shall be in pure doggy heaven the whole time I am there.

Next month I shall travel to Rome, where once again I have been invited to work with a group of people. All perfect for me because these locations are my favourite settings on the planet.

I want to show people how we can all take complete charge of our immediate situation by becoming harmonious within ourselves. This can work very quickly by using simple tools such as gratitude and decision making to shift our mental attitude from negative to positive in a very short time.

The more I follow this path I realise that it is not actually about being spiritual. Some people may view what I do as a very spiritual way of working, while others may prefer the quantum physics angle. I don't really want to put it into a box because one day I may work with someone who has a deep belief in God and another with someone who just wants to feel better about themselves. As far as I am concerned this is all fine. I just want each individual to get from this exactly what they need and what is right for them at any given time.

Over the centuries we have all been told what to think, what to believe and how to act by various political and religious bodies. I believe that now is the time for each and every one of us to completely reclaim our own individual power.

We need to be listening carefully to our own internal voice and making our own choices from deep within ourselves. This can then enable us to live life with complete joy and absolute freedom.

If, through my work, I can help those people who are seeking to find not only freedom but a deep connection to self, then I know I am accomplishing what it is I set out to do.

About the author/more information

Liz Vincent is a world class hypnotherapist, past life and this life regression specialist and healer, with practices in Harley Street, London, and Bristol, UK. She also travels and works with clients from all over the world, either in person or by telephone.

She holds a diploma in hypnosis, and senior membership with the General Hypnotherapy Register and General Hypnotherapy Standards Council. Liz is a trained past life regression therapist, and is a member of the Past Life Therapists Association and the International Association for Regression and Research Therapies. She also holds a diploma in Cognitive Behaviour Therapy.

Her other training includes Advanced Emotional Freedom Technique (EFT) with the Association of Meridian Energy Therapies, and with Gary Craig the founder of EFT. She is a Neuro-Linguistic Programming (NLP) practitioner with the American Board of NLP, an Advanced Theta Healer and Teacher, a Reiki Master, a Tachyon Practitioner, Eye Movement Desensitization Reprocessing (EMDR) Certified, EmoTrance Practitioner, Hypnosis for Childbirth Practitioner and Gastric Band Hypnosis Practitioner. She is also a member of the Spirit Release Foundation and is a fully qualified teacher of adults.

Liz is also a member of the Complementary and Natural Healthcare Council.

She has appeared on SkyOne Television, BBC Radio London, BBC Radio Bristol and in Cosmopolitan, New Woman, Prediction, Bon Marche and Time Out magazines. Soul & Spirit Magazine also chose to feature Liz in its *Tried & Tested* section.

If you would like some more information, or would like to experience hypnosis or some other form of treatment with Liz, please visit her website: www.awakening2hypnosis.com. You can also contact her by e-mail at liz@awakening2hypnosis.com, or by telephone at 0203 3972 513 or 07769 682383.

If you are telephoning from outside the UK please use +44 as the code for the UK leaving off the first zero from the numbers given above.

Recommended reading

Arntz, William and Vicente, Mark. (2007). *What The Bleep Do We Know?*. Health Communications

Bartlett, Dr Richard. (2009). *Matrix Energetics*. Beyond Words Publishing

Bradshaw, John. (1999). *Home Coming*. Piatkus Books

Brennan, Barbara Ann. (1990). *Hands of light*. Bantam

Browne, Sylvia. (2006). *Past lives, Future Healing*. Piatkus Books

Byrne, Rhonda. (2006). *The Secret*. Simon & Schuster Ltd

Cannon, Dolores. (2000). *Jesus and the Essenes*. Ozark Mountain Publishing

Chandler, Charlotte. (1995). *I Fellini*. Random House

Courteney, Hazel. (2004). *Divine Intervention*. CICO Books

Emmons, Robert Dr. (2008). *Thanks!*. Houghton Mifflin Harcourt

Fiore, Edith. (1995). *The Unquiet Dead*. Ballantine Books

Ingerman, Sandra. (2010). *Soul Retrieval*. HarperOne

Markham, Ursula. (2003). *Past-Life Regression*. Vega Books

McGill, Ormond. (1996). *Seeing The Unseen: A Past Life Revealed Through Hypnotic Regression.* Crown House Publishing

McGill, Ormond and Silver, Tom. (2003). *Hypnotism - A Hypnosis Training and Techniques Manual.* The Silver Institute Publishing Company

Newton, Michael. (1994). *Journey of Souls.* Llewellyn Publications

Newton, Michael. (2000). *Destiny of Souls.* Llewellyn Publications

Sheldrake, Rupert. (2009). *Morphic Resonance.* Park Street Press

Stibal, Vianna. (2010). *ThetaHealing: Introducing an extraordinary Energy Healing Modality.* Hay House

Tendam, Hans. (2003). *Exploring Reincarnation.* Rider

Weiss, Brian. (1994). *Many Lives, Many Masters.* Piatkus Books

Weiss, Brian. (2001). *Through Time into Healing.* Piatkus Books

Weiss, Brian. (2004). *Same Soul, Many Bodies.* Piatkus Books

Weiss, Brian. (1997). *Only Love is Real.* Piatkus Books

Weiss, Brian. (2000). *Messages from the Masters.* Piatkus Books